90 0777122 8

KV-482-520

PORT AND TERMINAL MANAGEMENT

WITHDRAWN FROM
UNIVERSITY OF PLYMOUTH
LIBRARY SERVICES

7 Day

University of Plymouth Library

Subject to status this item may be renewed
via your Voyager account

http://voyager.plymouth.ac.u

Tel: (01752) 232323

Ship

Distance Learning Programme
of
The Institute of Chartered Shipbrokers

Shipbroker A person having one of several occupations, chartering agent or owner's broker, negotiating the terms of the charter of a ship on behalf of a charterer or shipowner respectively; sale and purchase broker negotiating on behalf of buyer or seller of a ship; ship's agent, attending to the requirement of a ship, her master and crew while in port on behalf of the shipowner, loading broker, whose business is to attract cargoes to the ships of his principal.

Published and Printed in England by
Witherbys Publishing Ltd., 32-36 Aylesbury Street, London EC1R 0ET

Published for the Institute of Chartered Shipbrokers
First Published 2007

ISBN 978 1 85609 342 2

© Institute of Chartered Shipbrokers

UNIVERSITY OF PLYMOUTH
9007771228

British Library Cataloguing in Publication Data

Port and Terminal Management
  1. Harbours – Management 2. Marine Terminals –
  Management
  I. Institute of Chartered Shipbrokers
  387.1'068

ISBN-13: 9781856093422

© Copyright
All rights reserved. No part of this publication may be reproduced, stored in a retrieval system, or transmitted, in any form or by any means, electronic, mechanical, photocopying, recording or otherwise, without the prior permission of the publisher and copyright owner.

Notice of Terms of Use

While the advice given in this document ("document") has been developed using the best information currently available, it is intended purely as guidance to be used at the user's own risk. No responsibility is accepted by the Institute of Chartered Shipbrokers (ICS), the membership of ICS or by any person, firm, corporation or organisation [who or which has been in any way concerned with the furnishing of information or data, the compilation or any translation, publishing, supply or sale of the document] for the accuracy of any information or advice given in the document or any omission from the document or for any consequence whatsoever resulting directly or indirectly from compliance with or adoption of guidance contained in the document even if caused by a failure to exercise reasonable care.

Published and Printed by
WITHERBYS PUBLISHING LIMITED
32–36 Aylesbury Street,
London EC1R 0ET, England
Tel No. 020 7251 5341   Fax No. 020 7251 1296
International Tel No. +44 20 7251 5341   Fax No. +44 20 7251 1296
E-mail: books@witherbys.co.uk   Website: www.witherbys.com

THE QUEEN'S AWARDS
FOR ENTERPRISE:
INTERNATIONAL TRADE
2007

[5838]

THE INSTITUTE OF CHARTERED SHIPBROKERS

The Institute of Chartered Shipbrokers is the only internationally recognised professional body representing shipbrokers, ship managers and agents throughout the world.

With 24 branches in key shipping areas, 3,500 individual and 120 company members, joining ICS represents a commitment to maintaining the highest professional standards across the shipping industry worldwide.

In today's world it is essential for reasons of

- competitiveness
- efficiency and
- safety

that all key players understand the contractual relationships between themselves.

Staff with ICS qualifications subscribe to a common worldwide standard of professional competence and conduct. They have a thorough understanding of all aspects of shipping including law, insurance and economics and by doing so can communicate effectively with specialist professionals.

"ICS is the only source of professional and vocational qualifications in shipping. Take it from us, all other things being equal, the ICS qualified candidate will get the job."
Phil Parry, Managing Director, Spinnaker Consulting

Companies employing ICS qualified staff can be confident that they have played their part in ensuring that professionalism, industry knowledge and risk awareness are of paramount importance to their Board and management.

To find out more about ICS and membership either as an individual or company, please contact us at:

85 Gracechurch Street
London EC3V 0AA
UK
T: +44 (0)20 7623 1111
F: +44 (0)20 7623 8118
E: info@ics.org.uk

www.ics.org.uk

PREFACE

Professional education through TutorShip distance learning courses

The Institute of Chartered Shipbrokers (ICS) is the professional body for all concerned in the business of commercial shipping. Passing its examinations and being elected to membership (MICS) provides a successful candidate with the only internationally recognised qualification for shipbrokers.

The complete syllabus covers the following subjects:

Introduction to Shipping
Legal Principles in Shipping Business
Economics of Sea Transport and International Trade
Shipping Business

Dry Cargo Chartering
Ship Operations and Management
Tanker Chartering
Ship Sale and Purchase
Liner Trades
Port Agency
Port and Terminal Management

Shipping Law
Financial and Management Accounting
Logistics and Multi-modal Transport
Marine Insurance

The Institute believes it is essential that a qualified shipbroker has a thorough knowledge of certain profession-specific subjects plus a sufficient knowledge of the law, insurance, economics etc so that they can communicate with a specialist professional. This results in less confusion, misunderstanding and hopefully less contractual risk. Professionally qualified personnel are consequently ideally placed to undertake the key executive roles in the shipping service sector.

The true value of these course books is only gained if the student enrols on the TutorShip distance learning programme. We would suggest that there is nowhere better to turn to than ICS TutorShip courses for preparing yourselves for a highly successful career in the shipping profession.

We further recommend these books for practitioners and those already working in the Shipping Industry and allied trades. They will ensure you are kept abreast of developments as well as acting as useful everyday knowledge based texts for every aspect of this 'shipping business'.

Further details can be found at www.ics.org.uk

CONTENTS

Chapter 1

PORTS AND THEIR FUNCTIONS

1.1   INTRODUCTION

To the mariner, a port is a safe place for ships to load and unload freight and passengers. The emphasis is on safety from wind and weather, and from hull and bottom damage. Within a place of safety the commercial business of loading, unloading and replenishment of the ship is carried out. It can be performed either alongside a quay or at anchorage, using barges and tenders. The key requirement for the location of a port is the commercial demand for the movement of goods and people. It does not follow that a safe place will be a port, but a port must be a safe place. Ports have developed in locations where there is natural safety, but today if required, safe harbours can be constructed.

To the shipper or passenger, a port is the interface between land and water transport. Good land transport links are required, as are facilities for storing and handling goods and processing passengers. The use of a port is a cost burden to shippers of goods which could form a barrier to trade. Ports costs are kept as low as possible to encourage trade and stimulate port growth.

To the national economist, a port is a gateway to all the benefits of international trade. For this reason, governments will support and even subsidise their most important ports. Ports may be a gateway to less desirable activities such as smuggling and since the turn of the twenty-first century, terrorism.

To the port manager, the port is a business that can be used, if well managed to make profit. Poor management can lead to financial loss. In a national framework non financial objectives of a port may be of strategic importance.

Despite changes from a labour intensive technical intensive industry a port is a source of direct employment and indirect employment for the many enterprises associated with its activities.

A port has a variety of functions that meet the needs of its many stakeholders in different ways. Chapter One will explore the different types of ports and their functions. It will consider the place of a port in the context of international trade.

1.2   THE IMPACT OF PORTS ON ECONOMIC DEVELOPMENT

No country can produce everything that its own people need or want. However, by opening its borders to international trade a country gains far more than basic resources and exotic luxuries. Trade allows a country to concentrate production and specialise in those things that it does well, while buying in more cheaply those things that it does less well. It allows businesses to learn from the best in the world in terms of management skills and technology and it creates huge, world-wide markets to stimulate investment and innovation. Trade increases the wealth of nations, and ports are the gateway to trade. They are also, as a cost in the chain of transport, a barrier to trade.

If there is only **one port** serving an inland market, problems of high prices and inefficiency, typical of any monopoly can be created. High prices and inefficiency will have to be borne by all goods passing through the port. The effect is the magnification of costs to all industries using the port. The traditional answer to the problem is for the port to be owned by the state or alternatively by the local community, as a **trust port** in the United Kingdom. If the state owns the port, state inefficiency is added to the original problem of monopoly, so although prices are kept down inefficiency will still be a barrier to trade.

Lack of port capacity will also choke trade and affect the economic growth of the whole inland area served by the port, known as the **hinterland**. Congested ports mean long waits for a berth for the shipowner. Whilst waiting for a berth the shipowner will still have to pay their crews and other costs while earning nothing. The cost of congestion may be passed on to the shipper in the form of a surcharge. Extreme cases of congestion can lead to shipping lines boycotting a port.

Efficient ports having the capacity to meet demand and a rapid system of clearance of goods can drive down costs. Efficiency stimulates trade which leads to an increase in production volumes resulting in an increase in jobs and the development of new markets. The economic **multiplier effect**, is an important function of the port. Ports can be potential bottlenecks where free and rapid movement of goods across the interface can be slowed down by inefficiencies, particularly of an organisational nature.

Large ports are an ideal location for industries which are dependent on imported bulk raw materials, such as steel works and the petrochemical industry. Clusters of related industries tend to form around the primary industry. Storage and distribution centres tend to be located in or near to ports providing an opportunity to **add value** to the basic imported or exported good. Added Value activities include packaging, re-packaging, labelling, testing, tracking and tracing goods in transit and participation in organisational information flow.

1.3 THE EFFECT OF GLOBALISATION

Finance, trade, investment and production binds the world together. Governments are tied into free trade communities and organisations. Individuals may bind together in campaign groups. The consumer culture is spread across the globe through the media and the products of multi-national companies. This is globalisation, a process that is developing at growing speed. Cheap and efficient transport is one factor that both drives, and is driven by, globalisation. The impact on ports is immense.

The most obvious effect of globalisation is the **growth in world trade** which is increasing at a greater rate than world output. In real terms, the value of world exports has increased from $58,500 million in 1948 to $7,482,241 million in 2003. The majority of trade is in manufactured goods. (the volume of world merchandise exports increased by 2.5% in 2002, when trade as a whole only grew by 0.8%), and much of it is carried by sea in containers. Port capacity and port efficiency have developed to keep up with the growth in world trade

The **pattern of world trade** has changed due to the globalisation of world production and consumption. Manufacturing companies are able to move their factories to the Far East, where labour costs are a fraction of those in Europe and North America. Due to cheap transport by sea the goods can be shipped back to the markets in the West and profits made. Manufacturing itself can be divided with components made in several different countries, shipped to another for assembly and then shipped out across the world for sale.

Goods held in warehouses as **buffer stocks** close to the point of delivery are a cost for the manufacturer. Stocks tie up capital which can otherwise be invested in company expansion or the purchase of additional raw materials. Raw materials in storage ready to be fed into the production line can represent unnecessary cost. The Japanese pioneered the concept of the **just-in-time** process by which goods arrive at a point where they are needed just in time to be used. The just in time process cuts costs but without buffer stocks in place increases the vulnerability of the supply chain. Co-ordination between the parties involved including the supplier, customer and transport operator are essential to ensure that the just-in-time concept is effective.

Global markets lead to **competition** in a global dimension. Costs of goods are driven down by international competition. The pressure to reduce costs also impacts on the transport industry. In the mid nineteen sixties international shipping responded to rising costs through the development of unitised cargo systems, in particular the container. Time spent by a ship in port reduced from days or weeks into hours. Due to mechanisation fewer dock workers were needed. Recognising the efficiency that can be gained from **economies of scale**, ships of increasing capacity were built, a trend which continues to the present time. Mechanisation and economies of scale have meant that fewer crews are needed to move the same amount of goods. Increasing ship size has led to a need for larger and more efficient ports. Port efficiency can be improved through the effective use of information technology and computer system.

Inland transport, serving a port from the landward side has responded to pressure to become more efficient by the development – roads, rail and waterway systems. The hinterland of an individual port has grown and in some cases overlaps with adjacent ports. Ports have become increasingly competitive with each other. In North-West Europe, for example, Hamburg competes with Antwerp, Amsterdam and Rotterdam for container cargoes. Regional competition between ports also exists as between the ports of North-West Europe and ports located in the Mediterranean.

Ports are one step in the global supply chain. The **choice of a port** based on the cost of the port services alone, is not solely that of the ship owner Port choice is one factor taken into account when the total cost of the supply chain is considered. Rotterdam has gained prominence as the principle port in Europe because of its deep-water access, efficient terminals and road, rail and inland-waterway links to the heart of Europe.

Another effect of the total-supply-chain approach to costs is the development of **air cargo transport** and its impact on the movement of goods by sea. An important component of distribution costs is the finance involved in goods. In comparison to air transport cargo movement by sea is slow and less predictable. High value and perishable goods therefore tend to move by air leaving low value goods with limited time sensitivity, to be transported by sea. There are circumstances when sea transport can compete or cooperate with air transport to meet the demands required by the shipper. Physical handling and documentary clearance at the port interface are key elements which determine choice of transport mode to be used.

In recent years some port organisations have become **multinational companies**. For example the Port of Singapore (now PSA Corporation) has used its expertise to build, own and run terminals in Europe, India, China and East Asia. Other major port multinational companies include DR World and Hutchison Whampoa. Multinational ownership of ports has tended to raise the expectation of improved standards and higher efficiency in port operation. Improvement at one port or terminal has influence on others which can be copied and increase inter port competition.

1.4 PORT LOCATION

The **need for a port** arises from the economic need to transfer cargoes between land and water modes of transport. A port comprises of the sea approaches providing access and shelter, and land structures such as quays warehouses and administrative accommodation. A good natural port site will only develop into an effective commercial port if there is commercial demand In the South West of England there are many ideal port sites, but few succeed as commercial ports. For example, Falmouth has all the features for access and shelter but the hinterland generates limited cargo volumes insufficient to support a commercial cargo port.

The generation of cargo is critical to the development of a commercial port. Old ports evolved in conjunction with early urban settlements, often located at the lowest river crossing point. Ships were small and able to lie aground close to the settlement and transfer their cargo into and from wagons. As the settlement grew, demand for shipping services increased. The building of river berths and linear quays for the transfer of goods became a necessity. Increasing demand for cargo storage, increased ship size and building techniques associated with the industrial revolution encouraged the development of artificial docks. The demand of steamships to run to regular scheduled services saw the development of **closed dock systems**. As trade increased and ships grew bigger new docks were developed down river, towards the sea. The movement of port activity towards the sea is evidenced in most river ports. In London the Pool of London used to be the site where cargo transfer took place. Enclosed docks capable of meeting the demands of trade and shipping moved towards the Thames Estuary, now focussed at the Port of Tilbury. A new river berth container port, known as the London Gateway Project, presently in the planning stage is sited even further seawards and will ensure that London and the South East of England has the necessary capacity to meet future demands of the containerised shipping industry.

Old ports retain an historical advantage long after they become redundant due to the use of new technology. To help pay for down river development, **redundant historical docks** in the city centre, can be sold as prime development opportunities.

London, New York, Rotterdam, Hong Kong and Shanghai are **historical ports** having hinterlands which generate large cargo volumes. As commercial centres they have access to capital that allows them to build new facilities to meet modern needs and overcome natural disadvantages. The creation of a port may have arisen by **proclamation**. There are examples where governments have simply chosen sites for new ports and proclaimed their legal status as ports. The criteria for site choice can be complicated and may not be associated entirely with geographic or commerce expediency. Legal status as a port can produce demand and stimulate growth and further demand. With limited or no competition, ports established by proclamation can grow and flourish.

Ports may be built or developed to handle a single commodity for which there is steady demand. Nouadhibou, located in Mauritania, West Africa exists to export iron ore that arrives by train from inland sources. Kharg Island in the Gulf is a rocky limestone island which is the principal oil exporting port for Iran. Commodity ports need no significant population or hinterland to support them. Refinement of the commodity for efficient transportation may be undertaken at a commodity port. When demand for the commodity fails the port dies.

Increasingly, **modern port development** takes place on green and brown field sites where extensive cheap land is available, short length, deep water approaches are present and inland links to an extended hinterland are effective. The availability of skilled labour, a significant industrial infrastructure and the desire to ensure the environment is considered, are also features which are considered important.

1.5 PORT TYPES

Ports can be described either by geographical features or by operational activity.

1.5.1 Geographic Port Types

An understanding of the geographical site of a port gives some insight into its operating advantages and disadvantages. For example a costly and environmental concern is the need for maintenance dredging required by some ports but not others. Another example would be that shelter and deep-water provided by a mountainous fjord would lack the dense urban populations that generate cargoes. The most important geographical types of port are;

The Ria

The Ria is a drowned river valley, caused by a rise in sea level at the end of an ice age. The deepest water is found in the narrowest part of the ria where fast-flowing currents keep the sea bed clear. Sydney, Brest, San Francisco and Plymouth harbours are all examples of rias.

Tidal Estuaries

Low relief, tidal estuaries, including the Thames estuary giving access to London and the Elbe Estuary which leads to the port of Hamburg, can be dredged to provide a deep-water approach as the estuary bed is composed of loose, post glacial infilling.

Delta

The drowned delta of the River Rhine basin has allowed the development of three major European ports, Amsterdam, Rotterdam and Antwerp. As the speed of a river slows on meeting the sea, the silt laden water deposits its load. Sand banks are created. To maintain access to and from the ports, continuous dredging of deposited silt is necessary. New channels can be easily cut through the deposited silt and any dredged spoil can be used to provide new land for industrial port development

Coastal post-glacial submergence

Costal post glacial submergence followed by weather and river erosion have created geographical forms appropriate for port development. Southampton and New York are examples.

Artificial harbours

Artificial harbours can be created, by the use of extended walls into the sea. The walls are known as moles. Moles are expensive to build and maintain. Without regular dredging there can be a build-up of silt. An artificial harbour may have to be enlarged or the port abandoned, if it cannot accommodate the growth in ship size. Dover and Ijmuiden, in the Netherlands, are successful ports of this type.

Non-tidal river ports

Non-tidal river ports can be found on the River Amazon and Mississippi River. The river port will be subject to seasonal changes in water level and shifting channels.

1.5.2 Operational Port Types

Ports can be conveniently defined by their operational activities. However within a large port a wide variety of individual activities will be undertaken. Where each activity is served by a specialist terminal. The most important operational port types are:

Container Port

There are four main types of container ports; They are the Direct Call Port, the Hub Port, the Transhipment Port and the Feeder Port.

Direct Call Port

A direct call port comprises of a number of dedicated container terminals used for handling containers at very high throughput levels. Containers will be moved to and from the Direct Call Port by rail, road or barges.

Hub Port

A container port which acts as a focus for container movement, through the use of mainline containerships and feeder ships, A hub port allows for container distribution by sea within a significant geographical area.

Transhipment Port

A transhipment port is an interchange point enabling containers to be transferred between different mainline containerships, A limited number of containers may move inland.

Feeder Port

A feeder port is a small or medium sized port through which containers are fed to one or more Hub Ports in the immediate geographical area.

1.5.3 Multi-Purpose Ports

Despite the development of containerisation, other ports having less sophisticated facilities are to be found, these include Multi-Purpose ports and Fruit Ports

Multi-Purpose Port

Due to weak hinterland transport infrastructure some countries have not been able to take full benefit of opportunities associated with unitised cargo, particularly containers. The traditional Multi-purpose port is found in the North-South trades where trade volumes are small and ports cannot afford to build expensive container terminals. The multi purpose port will precede the development of more specialised port facilities

Fruit Port:

Specialist fruit ports/terminal exist for export and import. Handling techniques determine the precise structure of a Fruit Port. Palletised and general cargo handling techniques in conjunction with chilled warehouses and storage facilities are used. In recent years the use of reefer containers is having an impact on the traditional systems.

1.5.4 Bulk Ports

The movement of dry and liquid bulk commodities in seaborne international trade is significant. Specialist ports have been developed to act as the places of interchange between the sea and land modes of transport.

Liquid Bulk Commodity Ports

The most significant liquid bulk commodity ports are those used for the export and import of crude oil. They are referred to as Oil Ports. Export Oil Ports are found in areas of oil production such as the Gulf of Mexico and the Middle East whilst import Oil Ports are found in areas of consumption close by oil refineries, such as Milford Haven in South Wales. Very deep water is needed for Ultra and Very Large Crude Oil Carriers. Liquefied Natural Gas (LNG) is a growing bulk liquid cargo type that requires specialised discharge and storage facilities.

Non-oil cargoes handled as wet bulks including fruit juices and wine are normally handled at specialised terminals within a general port.

Dry Bulk Commodity Port

Bulk commodity export ports tend to specialise in a single commodity. Import ports may store and handle several commodity types, such as coal and iron ore.

Coastal Bulk Port

Most coastal traffic which is generated in North West Europe has a bulk characteristic. Coastal Ports are often specialised to handle a limited range of specific bulk cargo types including oil products, china clay, fertiliser and scrap metal.

1.5.5 Ferry Ports

Ferry ports are associated with the movement of passenger and freight carried on trucks and trailers and are integral to road networks.

1.5.6 Cruise Ship Ports

The development of the cruise ship business has brought with it a need for facilities for ships and passengers. Specialised Cruise Ship Ports may be built as ports of call or turnaround ports where demand is high. Where demand is limited, terminals will often be redesigned using old port infrastructure. The demands of cruise ship operation represent significant investment for a port.

1.5.7 Other Operational Port Types

Other operational port types, not concerned with either the transfer of commercial freight or passengers, are Naval ports and Fishing ports. Both have specific needs which are outside the scope of this book.

1.5.8 Function of Ports

A port can have several core functions. The functions are described as Traditional functions, Transport or transit functions, Industrial functions and Network functions. In any analysis of port functions the close inter-relationships between the stated functions needs to be made clear.

Traditional Functions of Ports

From the broadest perspective the seaport performs an important link in the total transport chain. The seaport provides a storage area or facilities for the storage of goods until they are transported to their destination. The storage function can range from a simple parking area for road vehicles to tank farms capable of holding millions of barrels of crude oil. Seaports are alternative locations for industry, particularly heavy industry and those associated with shipping.

Transport Functions of Ports

Not only do ports provide the essential link in the transport network, but also provide opportunity for the transhipment of goods. Transhipment concerns the transfer of goods between other modes of transport allowing goods to move to the final destination, which extends beyond the port. Transhipment can take place from the seagoing vessels to barges, railway wagons, road haulage vehicles or aircraft. Increasingly transhipment occurs between seagoing vessels. The transport function is characterised essentially by the transport mode used, which in turn is a function of the type of goods carried, the length of journey to be made and geographic conditions. The storage function of a seaport is directly related to its transport function. Seagoing vessels are many times larger than units of inland transport, so for transport overland the total cargo carried by the seagoing vessel has to be split into smaller consignments. The smaller consignments will be conveyed over a route which is determined by factors other than those which influence the need to dispose of the ship's total cargo as quickly as possible. The provision of storage space provides an obvious answer for perishable and non perishable goods which do not depend on onward shipping by sea transport.

The Industrial Function of a Port

The industrial function of a port is the logical offspring of its two other functions. The consideration that transhipment always involves handling costs as well as onward shipping in smaller, generally more expensive transport has induced many industries, notably those processing raw materials to locate in seaports. For a port to fulfil these various functions, facilities are needed for ships, waterways, harbour basins, berths for inland transport, canals, roads, railways, storage and industrial land. Such facilities call for large investments with a long life-time which influence the physical and economic health of the region.

Network Functions: Hub and Spoke Ports (the Load Centre Concept)

The increased use of containerisation in shipping has led to changes in the way that ports are used. Because of the need to exploit scale economies requiring large cargo volumes, ports serving the liner trades have become increasingly specialised. Two distinct types of port have emerged, the hub port and the feeder port. The hub port, sometimes known as a "load centre", acts as an important focus for container movement. The hub port is served by many ships and acts as a centre of cargo distribution to a wide geographic region which may reach beyond the national boundary of the port. A feeder port is of lesser significance, as cargo volumes are smaller. Economies of scale are not so easily exploited, so the routes a feeder port serves will be less busy with smaller vessels engaged on the route. A hub port will be at the centre of a local network of feeder ports creating a system which has been called "hub and spoke operation". Cargo is first moved to the hub and radiated out along the spokes, the arrangement is also observed in the world of air transport where it is used to exploit scale economies by using large aircraft to serve the hub and smaller ones on feeder routes.

The development of the hub port concept means that ports of the future may not necessarily need to have close hinterlands close to them. An example is the port of Algeciras which has little or no industrial development close by but is ideally located to act as a transhipment terminal where containers can be moved between vessels, reducing the shipping companies' overall costs. The importance of location as a determining factor for port development, particularly in the container trades is high. Location will determine the ports strategic importance to liner companies' route networks.

1.6   PORTS AND INDUSTRIAL DEVELOPMENT AREAS

Ports are located in areas where industrial and economic development can be encouraged. There are three recognised terms associated with such areas, namely the Free Port, MIDAS Ports and Industrial Development Zones.

1.6.1   Free Port

A Free Port, sometimes referred to as a Free Trade Zone or an Export Processing Zone is a port or a secure area within a port where customs dues are not payable and is intended to attract manufacturers and processors involved in domestic and export markets. Goods can be stored duty free and "value" can be added before the goods are re-exported. In a Free Port goods can be purchased duty free encouraging development The Port of Aden was an early example that used its Free Port status to attract shipping.

1.6.2   MIDAS Ports

Maritime Industrial Development Areas (MIDAS) were a popular concept in the 1960s in Europe when heavy industry moved to port sites. MIDAS were seen as a generator of industrial growth.

1.6.3   Industrial Development Zones

With heavy industry and manufacturing moving to the Far East a new form MIDAS in the form of an Industrial Development Zone (IDZ) has been created. The Industrial Development Zone has a similar function to the MIDAS encouraging economic growth in developing countries, but in an environmentally sustainable way.

1.7   CONTAINER TRANSHIPMENT

Economies of Scale are used in transport to reduce the cost per unit carried. Container ships are still increasing in size, with a container ship capable of carrying 13,000 containers (13,000 TEU) approved but not yet built. Container shipping companies continue to consolidate and concentrate their resources and services on a few, very large terminals. This has led to the development of the hub and spoke system in container shipping.

The hub and spoke system allows the container shipping company to choose to directly serve one or two ports at each end of the shipping leg. The ports, known as 'hub' ports, are the focus of regional container activity. Containers are transferred at the 'hub' ports into feeder ships for distribution to 'feeder' ports which lie at the end of 'spokes' radiating out from the hub. The operation also takes place in reverse with containers, loaded into feeder ships at feeder ports being carried to the regional hub port.

Singapore is an example of a major regional 'hub' port in the Far East. In North West Europe main line ship calls to a number of Direct Call Ports are normal. New, deep water 'hub' ports, strategically placed on the main East-West trade routes are being promoted as alternatives to the traditional Direct Call Ports. The Port of Algeciras in Spain is growing as a 'hub' port for European container operations.

Container transhipment is encouraged by the development of joint ventures between shipping companies and ports. Joint ventures help provide the finance for large scale infrastructure developments required of the industry. Increase in ship size requires deeper entrance channels, longer berths, larger gantry cranes, strengthened quay structures and additional yard storage space. Joint ventures may provide the opportunity to develop and enjoy the benefits of dedicated container terminals. With control of terminal and landside operations, a container shipping line can ensure that the cost advantages of very large ships are not lost through inefficiency at the port.

1.8   INTERMODALISM

The modern shipping container developed from a swap-body for trucks and rail. International containerisation was only possible after an internationally agreed standard for external dimensions was agreed. In 1965 the International Standards Organisation (ISO) agreed standard internal and external dimensions and weights for the freight container. The length of the container was based on a multiple of 10 feet with standards developed for 10 foot, 20 foot, 30 foot and 40 foot units. The 20 and 40 foot long container was adopted by the deep sea container ship operators. The external maximum width was established as 8 foot and height, the least problematical dimension, either 8 foot or 8 foot 6 inches. The International Standard allowed manufacturers to standardise the construction of equipment used for the movement of the container. International standardisation made the development of the containers system possible. The ability of the container to be transferred between different transport modes, **intermodalism**, is the cornerstone of an effective transport system. Intermodalism in combination with standard documentation and electronic data transmission allows a container shipping company to offer a door-to-door service and gives the ability to track and trace an individual container throughout its journey.

The container port is an important transfer point in the intermodal chain and one where delay can occur. To operate efficiently a port needs to minimise dwell time, the time an inbound or outbound container is stored at the port. **Dwell time** is a measure of port efficiency created by transport delays, documentary processes, customs demands and security clearance. A maximum dwell time of three days is considered sufficient in most circumstances.

Documentation between exporter, importer, shipping company, port and customs authorities is exchanged in electronic form using Electronic Data Interchange (EDI). Connections are established with the customs authorities using electronic network such as ATLAS, the system of the European Union. Outbound goods may receive customs clearance in advance. Some less developed countries do not have the ability to permit customs processing except at the port. Customs activity can create delay, risk the integrity of the door-to-door concept and reduce port capacity.

1.9   PORT OWNERSHIP

In the past ports were publicly owned. Public ownership protected port users from the abuse of monopoly power. In nations with poor capital markets, development works could be paid for with public money. It made sense for the public to own and manage their ports as a service to all the users, rather than allowing the port to be a private business where profits were distributed to shareholders and arguably at the expense of trade and the economy.

The late twentieth century saw a process of port privatisation occur in the United Kingdom. State owned ports and forced privatisation of former trust ports took place. Whilst such complete private ownership is rarely found elsewhere in the world, the concept of private operation and venture capital investment in port infrastructure has been recognised. Privatisation aims to increase port efficiency, free a port to raise money in the capital markets and reduce the size of the public sector financial commitment.

Activities within a port can be considered under three functions

The Port or Harbour authority

The port or harbour authority is a legally defined body responsible for the maintenance and development of the port infrastructure. It will have particular responsibility for port conservancy and will co-ordinate the many different activities that go on within the port.

Port Terminal Management

A large port will have dozens of different terminals within its limits, each specialising in a particular trade. Port terminals may be let to individual private companies who will define policy and manage activities associated with the terminal.

Service Functions

Service functions include activities such as stevedoring, pilotage and security. The functions will be managed by separate organisations who will be responsible for standards of management and service.

1.9.1   Types of Ownership

Ports are generally classified into one of the three types stated below.

Landlord Port

The landlord port is where the wet and dry infrastructure, is owned by the port authority, often a municipal or state body. The superstructure warehouses, buildings and handling equipment is owned by the private firms which leases the quay and its adjacent area. Private enterprise provides stevedoring and may also provide services including pilotage.

Tool Port

In a tool port the landlord provides both the infrastructure and the superstructure but not stevedoring facilities.

Service Port

The port authority owns and maintains all facilities in a service port. Port management offers the complete range of services necessary for the port to operate. The majority of ports in the developing world, are service ports.

The trend world-wide is for a state owned and run Service Port to be replaced by a port containing a mixed public private partnership. There is also a trend for publicly owned functions to be decentralised from government control, often through a government owned public corporation. Service ports have tended to be inefficient often through the use of excessive labour. Service ports have responded to political, rather than commercial pressure.

In the modern global economy there are fierce competitive pressures in the ports sector. Control of the immediate port hinterland has been broken by the development of motorways, railways, inland waterways and feeder ships. Private ownership provides ports with the discipline and flexibility to be able to compete in a competitive market place

1.10   SELF-ASSESSMENT AND TEST QUESTIONS

Attempt the following and check your answers from the text.

1. Explain what is meant by the hinterland of a port.
2. How does trade benefit a country?
3. Describe the impact of globalisation on port activity.
4. Discuss the most important criteria for port location.
5. What is a MIDAS port?
6. Discuss reasons for container transhipment.
7. Explain the importance of the intermodal concept.
8. Describe the purpose of port privatisation.

Having completed Chapter One attempt the following questions and submit both answers to your Tutor.

1. Discuss the role of ports in international trade and explain how ports can benefit or detract from the economic development of a country.
2. Choose a port in your country that you are familiar with, and explain the geographic and other features that affect its operation and success.

CARGOES AND SHIPS

2.1 INTRODUCTION

There are approximately 90,000 ships of more than 100 gross tons in the world fleet. Of these more than half are described as cargo carrying ships. The importance of the cargo carrying fleet is illustrated by the fact that it is 95% of the world fleet measured by gross tonnage. Presently the gross tonnage of the cargo carrying fleet will exceed 600 Millions gross tons The other sector of the world fleet includes services ships, vessels working in the offshore sector and fishing vessels

Chapter Two is concerned with the cargo carrying ship and the cargoes which are carried. It will provide an overview of the basic design of the more important ship types and consider the cargo characteristics which influence design. In addition it will provide a general overview of the major trade routes associated with world seaborne trade

2.2 CATEGORIES OF SHIP TYPES

Until the middle of the last century ships of the world cargo carrying fleet could be categorised very simply into one of three types; dry cargo ships, tankers and passenger ships. The shipping revolution which occurred in the latter half of the twentieth century led not only to an increase in ship size but also to the specialisation of ship type. Specialisation was principally based on the form of cargo carried.

Today more that fifty separate cargo carrying ship categories are detailed in Lloyds Register-Fairplay "World Fleet Statistics". They range from crude oil tankers to ships specifically designed to carry wood chips. A source of information which looks at the contemporary design of ships is the Royal Institution of Naval Architects annual publication "Significant Ships"

Bulk Liquid Ships: There are four principal types of ship within the category which are designed to carry liquid cargoes. They are the crude oil tanker the product tankers, liquefied gas carriers and the chemical carriers.

Bulk Dry Ships: The principal types of dry bulk ships include the general bulk carrier the ore carrier, the combination carrier and the self-discharging bulk carrier. They vary in size from small coastal bulkers to those engaged on trans ocean passages which may exceed 300,000 dwt (Deadweight tonne) The principal dry bulk cargoes carried are coal, iron ore grain and fertilisers. New ship designs allow the bulk carrier to accommodate the carriage of specialist cargoes including aggregates, cement and wood chips.

Other Dry Cargo Ships: Much seaborne trade concerns the carriage of manufactured and semi-processed goods, traditionally the preserve of the general cargo liner. Methods of cargo handling have encouraged the development of specialist ship types, the dominant of which are the cellular container ship, the Roll-On-Roll-Off ship and the reefer (temperature controlled cargo) vessel.

Passenger Ships: Whilst the traditional role of passenger ships providing liner services has changed since the end of the Second World War, their significance now lies in the ferry and cruise markets. Much innovation and development has taken place in the design of the ship and facilities offered to the passenger.

2.3 DESIGN OF SHIP TYPES

A ship is built to provide an income and profits for its owner. The design specification is initially established after consideration of the commercial need . Once the commercial need has been satisfied the naval architect will work on the design detail. The following commercial criteria are considered:

1. Market need

2. Commodity characteristics

3. Commodity weight, volume and value

4. Route distance

5. Trade route restrictions

6. Trade tonnage and contractual terms

7. Loading and unloading capability.

Market Needs

The factors which govern the basic design parameters of ship are based on a knowledge of present and future market demands for a specific trade. This could be for a specific commodity, such as liquefied natural gas or a more general trade, such as manufactured products.

Commodity Characteristics

Knowledge of the characteristics of the commodity or range of commodities to be carried by the specific ship need to be fully known and understood. Value, temperature sensitivity, fragility, odour and corrosiveness of the cargo may be among characteristics which govern the design of onboard storage capability and hence the design of the ship itself.

Commodity Weight Volume and Value

The characteristics of the cargo will include the relationship between volume of space required for a certain mass of cargo (known as the Stowage Factor). A high density cargo (low stowage factor) such as iron ore will bring the ship down to "her marks" long before space has been filled. The marks refer to the Loadline marks – a device originally developed by Samuel Plimsoll in the nineteenth century, and now contained in the Loadline Convention. The Convention not only details the Loadline marks but also ensures that the ship is built to provide minimum reserve buoyancy and hence protection against foundering in heavy seas. Cargo values vary. Regardless of value care has to be taken over its handling and storage. Crude oil is a cheap cargo compared to certain product oils. Contamination of the latter would lead to "off specification" and a reduction in value. Hence product tanker designs require a more sophisticated cargo containment and separation system than that of the crude oil tanker. In the dry cargo trades a car carrier provides an example of a ship designed to carry a high value, fragile and high stowage factor cargo with optimum capacity.

Route Distance

Cargo carrying ships are normally designed for world trading and ship designers need to consider size in relation to distance. In general the greater the route distance the more advantage can be gained by an increase in ship size (an economy of scale). Space for bunkers (ships fuel) and water ballast also needs consideration,

Trade Route Restrictions

The trade route itself will restrict the design of the ship. Port limitations (in particular depth of water), restrictions imposed by international canals and seaways (such as the lock size of the Panama Canal) and natural phenomena such as ice and sea conditions will have to be considered before design development begins.

Trade Tonnage and Contractual Terms

Trade tonnage also has an impact on the ship design. The total capacity of the route and the expectations of the merchant/shipper regarding service quality will have an impact on the design of the ship. The capacity of a trade route can be served by an infinite number of ship sizes and ship speed combinations. Speed of port throughput is also a factor. Prior to the replacement of general cargo liners by the container ship, the size of ships was severely restrained by the cargo handling capability. Increase in ship size and ship's speed took place but was incremental reflecting the slow growth in world trade. The design of large, higher speed ships combined with new cargo carriage and handling techniques has encouraged the development of trade by providing a system in which the cost element of transport for each commodity unit is small – Contractual terms using a "contract of affreightment" may require a shipowner to provide the delivery of a specific tonnage of cargo per period of time. An optimal design of ship will be sought to achieve such objectives. On passenger trade routes the development of high speed ferries has allowed two or more conventional ferries to be replaced by a single unit whilst still maintaining and sometimes allowing for increased route capacity.

Load/Unloading Capability

The safe carriage of cargo is of critical importance in the design of the ship, but also to be considered is the methods for unloading and discharging the cargo. Port turnaround time is of critical importance as a ship is only earning money when at sea. Recent innovations have helped ensure that the interchange of cargo between ship and port terminal is optimised. Port handling equipment (considered in Chapter Nine) is provided for use by ships which are not equipped with cargo handling systems. These ships are known as "gearless ships" and include iron ore carriers and cellular container ships. Port handling equipment may be used to supplement the use of ship's cargo handing systems. Ships which are equipped with cargo handling systems are known as "geared ships" and include smaller bulk carriers or general purpose vessels.

Design Spiral

Once the commercial concept has been considered and agreed a naval architect will be engaged to establish the specific ship design. One method of ensuring that the specific design is undertaken in a controlled manner is through the use of a design spiral, The design spiral provides an iterative and interactive process commencing with the commercial objectives outlined above and leading to more specific technical demands. Each stage has an influence on the final design. The technical demands within the design spiral include; cost estimates, ship stability, capacity, weight estimation, powering and propulsion methods, structural detail including scantling size, general arrangements, freeboard and subdivision, hydrostatics, ship lines and aesthetic proportions. Such detailed work has to be achieved within a complex international regulatory framework covering safety, environmental protection and accommodation standards. Additionally the rules of the Classification Society will also need to be considered.

2.4 CHARACTERISTICS OF CARGO

Loading, handling, stowage and discharge of cargo is normally undertaken by shore labour employed by the port or terminal, but working under the direction and supervision of the ship's officers. The Hague Visby Rules define the legal obligation of the ship to the cargo it carries. The Rules state that "the carrier shall properly and carefully load, handle, stow, carry, keep, care for and discharge goods carried". It is appropriate that all who are involved in cargo operations, including the port workers understand the characteristics of the cargo which they handle.

2.5   GENERAL CARGO

General cargo (sometimes known as break-bulk cargo), is a term used to describe non unitised cargo, traditionally carried on general cargo ships. General cargo is loaded and discharged piece by piece. General cargo tends to be of a maximum size and weight which can be man-handled. The term general cargo covers loose and packaged goods which may be consolidated into crates, cartons, bags, boxes, bales and drums. General cargo may be unitised, using pallets or containers to allow greater efficiency in transfer and transport. Heavy lift cargo, out of gauge cargo and small bulk cargo may also be referred to as general cargo. Equipment used for consolidating and moving general cargo is referred to as stevedoring equipment. Due to the many different characteristics of cargo handled, specialist equipment is necessary. Stevedoring equipment includes slings, strops, nets, and lifting boards, The equipment allows for the consolidation of cargo for lift-on, lift-off movement of between 1.5 and 5 tonnes. Slings, strops and nets are constructed of different materials including natural fibre rope, synthetic fibre rope, steel wire rope and chain. The choice of material used will depend upon the cargo type to be lifted. Lifting boards are normally made of timber.

Stevedores Equipment	Cargo Handled
Canvass Slings	Bagged Cargo
Loop Slings	Cases
Chain Slings	Logs: Steel Products
Rope Slings	Cases: Crates: Bags Packaged Timber
Wire Slings	Heavy Crates
Nylon Straps	Paper Rolls
Can Hooks	Drums
Plate Clamps	Metal Plate
Container Spreader	Containers
Grabs	Bulk Cargo

Figure 2.1 – General Cargo Stevedoring Equipment

Consolidation of cargo (using pallets) may be undertaken prior to the goods being delivered to the port terminal. Indivisible cargoes are those which require special handling, by heavy lift cranes provided either by the ship or port. Out of gauge cargo is that which is abnormal both in its dimensions and requirement for individual handling. A general cargo ship may carry small quantities of dry or liquid cargoes in bulk. When dry-bulk cargo is to be loaded or discharged the port will provide appropriate cargo equipment which is normally shoreside craneage with grabs. When liquid bulk cargoes are to be loaded or discharged an independent pumping system and flexible pipe line will be required.

2.6   UNITISED CARGOES

Unitisation is the word which expresses the consolidation of general cargoes into a unit form for ease efficiency of handling. Unitised systems are used throughout the transport system to enable greater efficiency of the prime transport vehicle to be achieved and to reduce the amount of handling of individual cargo items. Unitisation of the general cargo operation began in the mid nineteen sixties initially using methods of pre-slinging. This Chapter will look at the three methods used for the unitisation and consolidation of cargo

1.   Freight container

2.   Pallet

3.   Pre-slung

2.6.1   Freight Containers

The container is defined as *"an article of transport equipment of a permanent c*
accordingly strong enough for repeated use, specially designed to facilitate the
goods by one or more means of transport without intermediate reloading, designed t
and or readily handled having corner fittings for these purposes and of a size such that they are
enclosed by the four outer bottom corners is either at least 14 m² or at least 7 m² if it is fitted with
top corner fittings". The dimensions of the ISO Series 1 Freight Container are based on a 10 foot
length. The container length normally used by international shipping are either 20 or 40 feet.
Non standard container lengths have been established on some international trade routes,
with the 45 foot container being the most popular. The external width for all containers is 8 feet.
ISO Series 1 container height is either 8 feet or 8 feet 6 inches. High cube containers, having
a height 9 foot 6 inches are now common.

The strength of a container lies in the steel framework, which has to withstand the static and
dynamic loads which affect the container in transit. The cargo is protected by the floor, side,
end walls and the roof. The floor is made of timber protected by bitumen, while materials used
for the construction of walls and roof will be either mild steel, aluminium sheet or combined
plywood and glass reinforced plastic. Entry into a general purpose container is through a set
of full width and height rear doors. All freight containers are built and maintained to the
standards required by the International Maritime Organization's International Convention for
Safe Containers (1972)

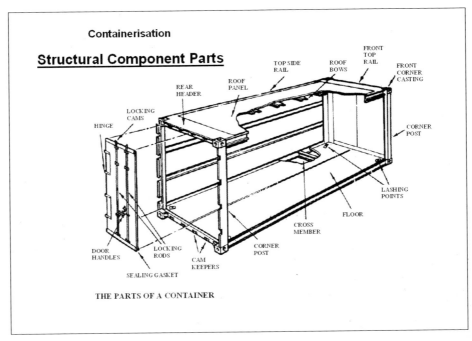

Figure 2.2 – Structural Component Parts of a Freight Container

The tare weight of the container will have an impact on the load which can be carried. The
tare weight of a container is the weight of the container excluding cargo and lashings. For a
20 foot container built of mild steel the tare weight will typically be 3 tonnes. Payload is the
weight of the cargo carried in tonnes. The gross weight is the tare weight plus the payload.
The maximum gross weight allowed for a 20 foot ISO Series 1 freight container is 20 tonnes
and that for a 40 foot ISO Series 1 container, 30 tonnes. The majority of containers carrying
manufactured goods are volume rather than weight limited. The strength of a container is built
into the corner posts. The corner posts have to be of sufficient strength to withstand a top loading
of eight containers of maximum gross weight without deflection.

The standard general purpose container is not appropriate for the consolidation of all types of cargo. To ensure different cargoes can be efficiently carried a range of containers derived from the standard container have been developed. They include, the half height container, the open sided container, the open top container, the bulk container, the flatrack, the tank container and the refrigerated (reefer) container. The reefer container carries its own refrigeration machinery and will require electrical supply by the port terminal to ensure the cargo is maintained within the desired temperature range.

Container Type	Typical Cargoes
Open Top	Can be loaded from the top. Suitable for bulky heavy goods e.g. coiled steel, electrical transformers
Flat Rack	Used for over height and over width cargo e.g. plant and machinery
Ventilated	Used for goods which need ventilation e.g. cocoa beans
Bulk	Used for free flowing solids e.g. granules, grains and powders in bulk
Reefer/Insulated	Used for cargoes which require to be carried at controlled temperatures e.g. dairy products, meat , photographic film
Tank	Used for liquid goods. Usually designed with a particular commodity in mind e.g. anti knock compound, beer
Half Height	Used for high density low volume goods e.g. steel plate, ingots, steel section
Open Side	Used for goods which need to be loaded from the side yet need maximum weather protection e.g. fruit vegetables and livestock

Figure 2.3 – Derivatives of the basic ISO freight container

There are more than 20 million containers in existence. All containers basically look the same. To identify an individual container a set of markings are carried on the roof, end door and sides. Identification by the port operator of an individual container is essential. Container identity marks are shown in Figure 2.4.

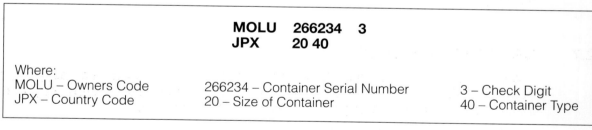

Figure 2.4 – Container Identity Marks

2.6.2 Pallets

A pallet is defined by the British Standards Institute (BSI) as *"a load board with two decks separated by bearers, blocks or feet, or a single deck supported by bearers blocks or feet constructed with the view to transport and stacking. It will have an overall height reduced to the minimum compatible with the handling of fork-lift trucks and or pallet trucks".*

There are a wide variety of pallets used by industry. The type most commonly found in port operations is the "transit" pallet which has an approximate life in normal use of 5 years. The transit pallet can be built in a number of ways to accommodate the compromise between "cost and utility". Issues concerning cost involve the type and amount of material used and the complexity of construction. The utility of a pallet is concerned with weight, reversibility, entry and lifting need. Pallet types concern two or four way fork entry, single or double-decking, and open or closed boards. A particular type met in port operations is the wing pallet, which permits lifting by the use of pallet spreaders. Pallets are produced in sizes to meet national and international standards. They may also be produced to meet specific warehousing or stevedoring operations The International Standard Organisation (ISO), standard size, known as "Europallet" has base dimensions of 1000mm x 1200mm (40" x 48") The British Standard Institute produces a standard base dimension of 1100 mm x 900mm (44" x 35.5") which provides optimal loading within an ISO Freight Container. The pallet height will vary between 100mm (4") and 150 mm (6") depending upon the construction, method and material employed.

The pallet is built to a rating which ensures it has the strength to withstand a nominal load when placed at the bottom of a four tier stack of laden pallets. The normal ratings are 1.0 tonne, 1.5 tonnes and 2.0 tonnes. A variety of ways are used to secure cargo to a pallet including the use of lock patterns of stowage, nylon web or steel band strapping, glue or nets. Cargo on a pallet may also be shrink wrapped with plastic film to ensure further security, protection against the weather and enhancement of identity. Pallets may be used in conjunction with containers and general cargo operations. They may also be used as an individual unit with the total supply chain, as for example in the fruit trades.

2.6.3   Pre-Slung cargo

Pre-slinging of cargo can be defined as "the process whereby a sling is placed around a cargo at the point of origin and remains in place on the transport unit for all or most of its subsequent journey, for the purpose of reducing the time spent in cargo handling operations" Pre-slinging of cargo was used in the liner trades at the time of the transition from general cargo to unitised operations and is still seen in coastal trades dealing with minor bulks. It is not a fully intermodal method of cargo movement.

Various types of sling are used. Originally natural fibre rope was used, but today flat synthetic web material, having a lifespan of between two and four years, is commonplace. Pre-slung cargo uses slings in the form of strops, loop slings, cloverleaf slings and bag slings.

Cargoes most suitable for pre-slinging include bagged cement, bagged fertilisers, forest products (such as timber deals, and sheet plywood) and construction materials. Compared to standard general cargo operations, pre-slinging allows a more efficient use of the ship, with reduced cargo handling costs and improved accounting (tallying) of the cargo loaded and discharged. Pre-slinging is cheap to implement and cargo operational control remains with the ship.

2.7   DRY BULK CARGOES

A dry bulk cargo is defined as "a homogeneous unpacked cargo such as grain, iron ore or coal" (Brodie). A dry bulk cargo has various characteristics which may impact upon loading/discharge and storage. Dry bulk characteristics include:

- Stowage Factor.

- Angle of Repose.

- Moisture Content.

Stowage Factor Is defined as the ratio of the cubic measurement to its weight and is expressed in cubic metres per tonne. For example iron ore has a stowage factor of about 0.33 cubic metres/tonne. Hay has a stowage factor of about 4 cubic metres/tonne.

The **Angle of Repose** of a bulk cargo is defined as the angle the natural slope of the commodity makes to the horizontal. Iron ore has an angle of repose of about 35°. Grain has an angle of repose in the order of 15°. A cargo with a low angle of repose, such as grain, needs to be levelled off to prevent surface movement when at sea

Moisture Content. Most dry bulk cargoes contain moisture. Excess moisture in a bulk cargo can cause the cargo to act as a liquid. This poses a danger to the ship. Before loading a dry bulk cargo the shipper has to declare to the ship's Master the moisture content of the cargo. Dry bulk cargoes have other characteristics which will have an influence their handling and stowage which include, flammability, friability, corrositivity, flowability, dust nuisance, biological activity, abrasiveness and thixotropocity.

2.8   LIQUID BULK CARGOES

A liquid bulk cargo is defined as *"unpacked homogeneous liquid cargo, such as crude oil, palm oil or liquefied natural gas"*. Liquid bulk characteristics include:

- Density.

- Temperature.

- Viscosity.

The density and temperature of a liquid bulk cargo will determine the volume it occupies. **Density** (specific gravity) is defined as *"the ratio the weight of a volume of liquid substance at its actual temperature bears to the weight of an equal volume of pure water at a fixed temperature"* (Packard). As the **temperature** of bulk liquid increases its volume will increase. Likewise when the temperature of the cargo falls its' volume will decrease. Allowance has to be made for the change of volume in the stowage of a liquid bulk cargo. Additionally the actual temperature of the bulk liquid cargo on loading/discharging needs to be known to establish its mass at a standard temperature and pressure. The **viscosity** of a liquid describes its resistance to move. A liquid cargo with a high viscosity is less easy to move than one with a low viscosity. Viscosity can be reduced by heating. Liquid Bulk cargoes have other characteristics which need to be considered including flammability, toxicity, vapour pressure and corrositivity.

2.9   TRADE ROUTES

Trade routes are the spatial highways between ports along which goods are moved from areas of excess supply to areas of demand. Seaborne trade routes are not static, they vary over time, with the discovery and development of new technology. It is impossible to describe all but the most defined trade routes which dominate today's international shipping industry.

2.9.1   Bulk Liquid Trade Routes – Crude Oil

Crude Oil is the largest commodity in terms of tonnage moved by seaborne trade. In 2003 in excess of 1,600 million tonnes were carried by tanker. There are three main exporting regions namely, the Middle East, North and West Africa and North of South America (Venezuela). Crude oil tankers collect crude oil from the export regions and transport it over many thousand of miles to refineries located in Europe, the United States of America, Japan and South East Asia. The map below (Fig 2.5) shows the general pattern of the seaborne movement of crude oil.

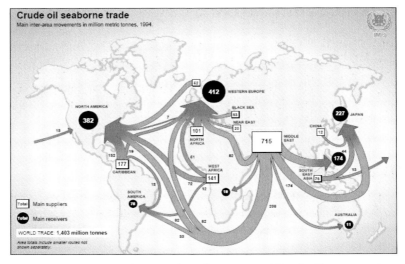

Figure 2.5 – Crude Oil: Seaborne Trade Routes

(Source: UN Atlas of the Oceans – on line)

At the refinery the crude oil is converted into petroleum products which are distributed to meet demand. As crude oil does not have a homogeneous character and refinery demand will vary, some unusual trading patterns will result, for example North Sea crude oil being transported to the United States of America

2.9.2   Bulk Dry Trade Routes – Coal

Coal fuelled the nineteenth century industrial revolution and is still a very important commodity in world trade. More than 550 million tonnes of coal is carried each year in seaborne trade making it the second largest commodity in world trade. Two major types of coal are moved in world trade. **Coking coal** is used in steel production and **steam coal** used by coal fired power stations to generate electricity. More than twice as much steaming coal is moved by sea transport than coking coal. The growth rate at the turn of the twenty-first century for steam coal is second only to liquefied natural gas – Coal is exported by sea from several main regions in the world of which Australia is dominant. The United States of America, Russia and South Africa are also significant providers of coal to world markets. The world's major import regions are the Far East, including Japan and China and Western Europe. The map below (Fig 2.6) shows the general pattern of seaborne trade in coal.

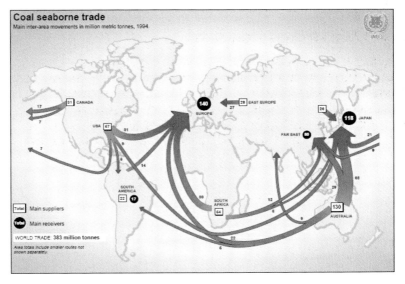

Figure 2.6 – Coal: Seaborne Trade Routes

(Source: UN Atlas of the Oceans – on line)

2.9.3 Bulk Dry Trade Routes – Iron Ore

Iron Ore is the necessary component required for the production of steel. Steel is a fundamental construction material. Demand for steel and hence iron ore reflects the world economy. Iron ore is the second largest bulk commodity moved in seaborne trade in recent years. Growth in the demand for iron ore has been significantly influenced by the demands of China. Whilst iron ore can be found in many areas of the globe, significant deposits of economic worth are mined in Australia and South America. Other export areas of iron ore include South Africa, West Africa, United States of America, Canada, India and Scandinavia. The dominant importers of iron ore include Europe and the Far East, including Japan and China. The map below (Fig 2.7) shows the general pattern of seaborne trade in iron ore.

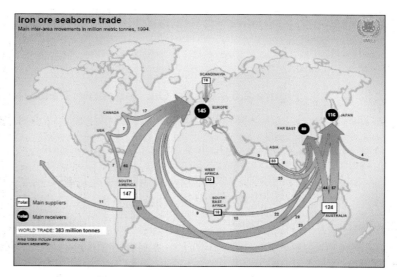

Figure 2.7 – Iron Ore: Seaborne Trade Routes

(Source: UN Atlas of the Oceans – on line)

2.9.4 Bulk Dry Trade Routes – Grain

Grain is the third largest dry bulk commodity moved by sea. In quantity terms it is of less importance than the other major bulk cargoes. The annual amount of grain which enter world seaborne trade exceeds 200 million tonnes although year on year demand will vary depending on harvest yields.

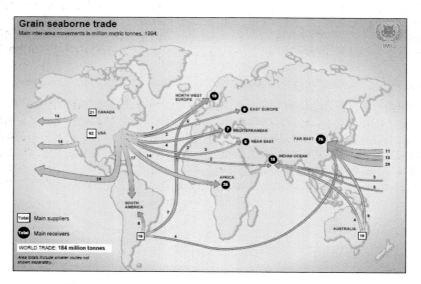

Figure 2.8 – Grain: Seaborne Trade Routes

(Source: UN Atlas of the Oceans – on line)

There are three regions of the world which produce excess grain for export, namely the United States of America, (the "world's granary") South America and Australia. There are many importing countries but Africa, India, the Far East and Europe are the main beneficiaries. The seaborne pattern of trade in grain is indicated on the map (Fig 2.8).

2.9.5 Liner Trade Routes

Liner trade routes are established by dominant trade flow of manufactured goods from areas of production to areas of consumption. The East West pattern is dominant although there is continuing growth in the North South trades. The trade routes link the major manufacturing and population areas of the world.

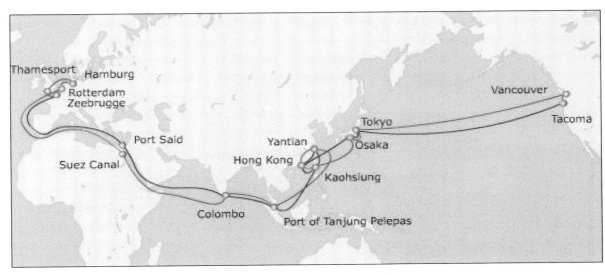

Figure 2.9 – Container Trade Routes
Europe – Asia – West Coast America

(Map: Evergreen Corporation 2006)

Whilst different services are provided by the container companies the dominant liner trade routes link Europe to the Far East to the United States of America to Europe. The development of the container trades has been rapid. Between 1986 and 2005 growth in containers carried averaged 9% per year. In 2003 the tonnage carried in containers was 723 million tonnes. Problems in the container trades concern imbalances of trade which create difficulties in positioning loaded and empty containers. Optimising the position of empty containers and special containers is a critical issue in efficiency. The development of China as a major manufacturing nation (43% of the world's output of motorcycles and 40% of colour televisions are presently made in China), has had a major influence on liner trades.

2.9.6 Cruise Ship Operating Areas

Whilst the cruise ship industry is small in terms of ship numbers it is one of the most rapidly growing areas in the shipping business. With the rare exception of "round the world" cruises, cruise ships are scheduled to operate in specific areas of the world, which provide an opportunity for a new stay each day with passage between ports being undertaken mainly at night. The best known cruise ship areas of operation are the Mediterranean, Caribbean, West Coast of United States, Canada and Alaska, Europe and South East Asia.

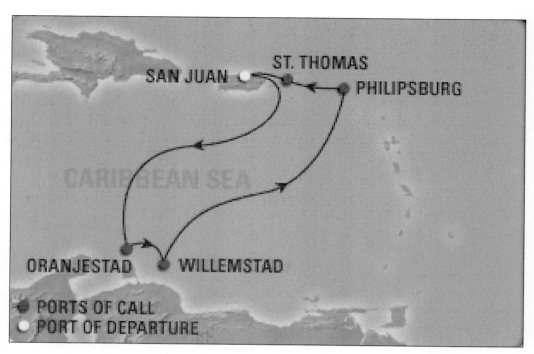

**Figure 2.10 – The Caribbean Cruise Ship Operational Area
(showing a typical seven day cruise pattern)**

(Map: RCCL 2006)

2.10   DISTANCE AND VOYAGE TIMES

A working knowledge of distance and voyage times between places of origin and destination is of importance to any person involved in shipping.

Port	Port	Distance (nautical miles)	Time (days & hours at 15 knots)
Atlantic Ocean			
Liverpool	New York	3171	8d 19h
London (Thamesport)	Gibraltar	1313	3d 15h
London (Thamesport)	Panama	4725	13d 03h
London (Thamesport)	Capetown	6110	16d 23h
New York	Capetown	6785	18d 21h
Buenos Aires	Capetown	3780	10d 12h
Buenos Aires	Magellan Straits	1275	3d 13h
Gibraltar	Port Said	1915	5d 08h
Indian Ocean			
Suez	Aden	1310	3d 15h
Capetown	Singapore (Tanjung Pelepas)	5650	15d 15h
Capetown	Freemantle	4961	13d 18h
Aden	Melbourne	6450	17d 22h
Aden	Singapore (Tanjung Pelepas)	3640	10d 02h
Pacific Ocean			
Singapore	Yokohama (Tokyo)	2888	8d 00h
Yokohama (Tokyo)	Sydney	4379	12d 03h
Yokohama (Tokyo)	Vancouver	4194	10d 15h
Yokohama (Tokyo)	Panama	7680	21d 08h
Sydney	Panama	7875	21d 21h
Sydney	Vancouver	6390	17d 18h

Figure 2.11 – Distance and Times Between Significant Ports of the World

The relationship between distance, time and speed is of importance to the ship's operator so that from a known departure time an Estimate of Arrival Time (ETA) can be established. Times on trans – oceanic routes are measured in days and hours. In practice distance and voyage times can be found using voyage estimation commercial software. Distances are based on a set of tables compiled by British Petroleum known as the 'BP Distance Tables'. In addition to knowledge of time required on passage, time zones will need to be considered to provide correct estimates of arrival. Figure 2.11 shows certain distances across the major oceans of the world and between some well known ports. The time it takes for the passage to be accomplished by a ship steaming at 15 knots is also stated.

The ships described in the next section are required to be self-sufficient in fuel, victuals and spares to cover the distance and time on passage between ports of departure and destination. Allowance has to be made for adverse weather and sea conditions.

2.11 SHIP TYPES

The section considers the basic types of ship used in world seaborne trade. The categories include the bulk liquid ship, the dry bulk ship, the ships designed to carry general cargo including the cellular container ship and roll-on, roll-off ship and passenger ships.

2.12 LIQUID BULK SHIPS

The liquid bulk ship is designed to carry bulk liquid cargoes. The variety of liquid bulk cargoes are extensive and range from crude oil to wines and molasses.

The dominant bulk liquid ship types are:

- Crude Oil Tankers

- Product Tankers

- Chemical Tankers

- Liquefied Gas Tankers

Crude Oil Tanker

The crude oil tanker is designed to carry the raw material of the petroleum industry from producing country to refinery normally located in the country of consumption crude oil tankers are classified by size of cargo mass which can be carried – known as the deadweight tonnage (dwt)

Size Classification of Crude Oil Tankers

Ultra Large Crude Carrier (ULCC)	300,000 dwt +
Very Large Crude Carrier (VLCC)	200,000 dwt – 299,999 dwt
Medium Size Crude Carrier	70,000 dwt – 199,000 dwt

The crude oil tanker is a single deck ship which under recent regulations has to have a double side and bottom structure referred to as "double hull". The accommodation and engine room are located aft with the cargo working deck and tank structure forward. The cargo tanks are created by two bulkheads running fore and aft, creating wing tanks and centre tanks. Transverse bulkheads subdivide the structure from fore to aft. A typical VLCC may have as many as 27 tanks. Tanks sizes are limited with the maximum size permitted capable of carrying 30,000 tonnes. A separate cargo pump room is positioned in the cofferdam space forward of the engine room. In addition to the cargo containment system, the crude oil tanker consists of a series of systems which allow the safe loading, carriage and discharge of the cargo. On deck and under deck pipeline systems are used to distribute and draw oil from the cargo tanks. Cargo valve systems are used to control the flow rate and distribution of the cargo. Cargo pumps, normally of a centrifugal type are used for discharge. Pumps may individually have a pumping rate exceeding 6000 tonnes per hour, Crude Oil Washing (COW) systems are used for tank cleaning and Inert Gas Systems (IGS) used to eliminate the accumulation of explosive gases. The structure of a cargo tank is protected from excessive pressure or partial vacuum, by a ventilation system which incorporates a Pressure Vacuum (PV) valve. A fire-fighting system using foam extinguishing medium is provided on the working deck. The control of the load and discharge operation is undertaken in a control room which has the capability for the remote operation of cargo valves and the distant reading of cargo tank information.

Figure 2.12 – Crude Oil Tanker at the Discharge Terminal
VLCC berth Maasvlakte terminal Rotterdam

(Photo: P. Wright)

Figure 2.13 – Liquefied Natural Gas Carriers

Product tanker

The product tanker has been developed to carry the refined product, which includes gasoline, diesel oil and fuel oil, from refinery to a port distribution terminal. Product tankers are smaller in size than tankers used to carry crude oil. The normal size ranges between 3,000 dwt and 40,000 dwt. The product tanker has many of the structural features of a crude oil carrier. The carriage of oil products has to be undertaken with particular care if more than one type of product is being carried. Contamination between cargoes can be costly. In recent new builds the pump room has been eliminated. Each individual tank is served by a deepwell pump. The new system significantly reduces the risk of cargo contamination.

Chemical Carrier

A chemical tanker has much in common with the product tanker. Due to the demand for the carriage of a wide range and quantity of different bulk chemical cargoes the ship will have greater subdivision of cargo tanks. The size and location of the cargo tanks will vary with those designed to carry noxious and toxic cargoes being placed in a protected position. Some chemical carriers have free standing 'on deck' tanks. Tanks are constructed of stainless or mild steel. Mild steel tanks will use epoxy, zinc silicate or rubber based coatings to protect the ship's structure from the cargoes carried. Chemical carriers have a double hull structure. On new tonnage individual tanks will be served by a dedicated deepwell pump. In addition tanks may be provided with cargo heating equipment. Ventilation systems are closed loop systems which eliminates the venting of dangerous gases to the atmosphere. The carriage of a wide range of chemicals poses dangers of reaction between incompatible types of cargo, risk of fire, explosion and potential danger to human health. Codes for the *Construction and Equipment of Ships Carrying Dangerous Chemicals in Bulk (the BCH Code and IBC Code)* have been developed by the International Maritime Organization. The International Chamber of Shipping's *"Tanker Safety Guide" (Chemicals)* provides guidance for operation of this ship type.

Liquefied Gas Carrier

Two types of gases are carried in liquefied form. Liquefied Natural Gas (LNG and Liquefied Petroleum Gas (LPG). The cargo containment system for LNG is always fully refrigerated whilst systems designed for the carriage of LPG may be fully refrigerated, fully pressurised or semi-pressurised and semi-refrigerated. The liquefied gas ship is complex to operate, but its safety record is exceptionally good.

2.13   DRY BULK SHIPS

The dry bulk ship is designed to carry those cargoes which are not loaded in separate packages, such as coal, iron ore and grain. Dry bulk ships are categorised by size and purpose.

The dominant dry bulk ship types are:

- General Purpose Bulk Carrier

- Ore Carrier

- Open Type Bulk Carrier

- Self Discharging Bulk Carrier

- Combination Carrier

Size (Deadweight tonnes)	Classification
10,000 – 49,999	Handy
50,000 – 79,999	Panamax
80,000 +	Capesize

Figure 2.14 – Size Classification of Dry Bulk Carriers

(Source: Intercargo 2006)

General Purpose Bulk Carrier

The general purpose bulk carrier is designed to carry many different forms of bulk cargo from timber to grain. The ships are simple vessels which have up to six undivided cargo holds forward of the accommodation and engine room. They are of single deck construction. The design of the general purpose bulk carrier ensures that she can load to her marks when carrying cargo regardless of the Stowage Factor. She is able to sail with propeller immersed when in ballast condition. The cargo holds are self trimming. Minimum obstructions such as pillars help ease the loading and discharge of the cargo. Access to the hold is by way of wide hatch ways and mechanically operated hatch covers. General purpose bulk carriers are usually equipped with their own cranes and grabs for loading and discharging in which case they are referred to as "geared" ships. Ballast water may be carried in upper and lower wing tanks

Ore Carrier

The ore carrier is a bulk carrier specifically designed to carry iron ore, a cargo with a high density and low stowage factor. The volume of space occupied by a cargo of iron is approximately one third the amount of space required by grain. The ore carrier will commonly have nine holds The cargo hold will be central to the structure with wing tanks providing space for ballast. A deep double bottom tank below the cargo hold will raise the centre of gravity of the cargo providing a less stiff ship and reducing structural stress. Strong longitudinal girders are provided to counteract bending moments and stresses in the fore and aft line of the ship.

Figure 2.15 – General Purpose Handysize Bulk Carrier
In ballast departing Rotterdam

(Photo: P. Wright)

Figure 2.16 – Iron Ore Carrier Arriving at Port Terminal
Arrival at Rotterdam to discharge cargo

(Photo: P. Wright)

Open Type Bulk Carrier

The open type of dry bulk carrier provides a box shaped hold with wide hatchways often exceeding 90% of the ship's width, The hull structure is described as being of box girder form. Such ships are designed to carry dry bulk cargoes and when required containers or uniform deals of timber.

Self-Discharging Bulk Carrier

The self-discharging bulk carrier refers to a limited number of bulk carriers which are equipped with specialised bulk handling equipment for continuous discharge operations. Self-discharging equipment includes the conveyor and discharge boom system. Pneumatic self-discharge systems may be used for powdered bulk cargo. The equipment is integrated into the design of the ship. The self-discharging category does not usually refer to bulk carriers which have conventional crane or derrick rigs. The self-discharging bulk carrier was developed for movement of cargoes on the Great Lakes of North America.

Combination Carrier

The combinations carrier has been designed to ensure maximum employment opportunities in fluctuating markets. Essentially the combination carrier is able to switch between the dry and wet bulk markets. Subcategories of combination carriers include the:

- OBO   Oil Bulk Ore Carrier

- O/O   Oil Ore Carrier

- PROBO   Product Oil Bulk Ore Carrier

The combination carrier is of similar structure and layout to the bulk carrier but has additional features to cope with oil cargoes. They have not been highly successful in operation due to the high costs associated with conversion between the carriage of dry and liquid bulk cargoes.

Other Specialised Bulk Carriers

Greater amounts of dry bulk cargo carried in world trade are leading to an increased specialisation of the dry bulk ship designed to accommodate specific cargo types. Categories of specialist dry bulk ships include the aggregate carrier, alumina carrier, cement carrier, limestone carrier, mud carrier, powder carrier, refined sugar carrier, urea carrier and wood chip carrier.

2.14 GENERAL CARGO SHIPS

General cargo ships are vessels designed to carry a wide range of cargoes from break-bulk to heavy lifts. Prior to the container revolution, general cargo ships provided liner cargo services for world trade, while still numerically the largest category of ship type, the average general cargo ship size is about 3,000 gt.

Sub categories of the general cargo ship include:

- Multi-Purpose ship

- Refrigerated (Reefer) ship

- Short Sea Coastal/River – Sea Ship

Multi-Purpose Ship

The multi-purpose ship is a decked vessel designed to carry bulk, break-bulk and unitised cargoes. Typically 15-20,000 gross tons in size and fitted with load and discharge gear, such ships are used in areas of the world where there is limited demand or poor inland transport infrastructure.

Refrigerated (Reefer) Ship

The refrigerated ship, often known as a Reefer ship, is designed to carry temperature sensitive cargoes, such as fruit, dairy products and meat. Reefer ships have traditionally used pallets in their loading discharge operation. There is an increasing use of refrigerated (reefer) containers in the cool trades.

Short Sea Coastal/River – Sea Ship

The use of smaller ships to distribute cargoes to both small coastal ports and river ports is growing in importance as industrialised nations seek to reduce the impact of congestion caused by road transport. Ships of this category are of various designs, often single hold and principally used either as container feeder ships or small bulk carriers. The size varies but is commonly between 1,500 dwt and 5,000 dwt. The design of short sea coastal and river – sea ships has to consider many factors including navigable draft and air height for river navigation.

2.15 CONTAINER SHIPS

The carriage of containers in deep sea trades was enabled by a revolution, which culminated in ships designed about a standard cargo unit, the ISO freight container. The cellular container ship dominates the liner trades used for the movement of processed and semi-processed goods in world seaborne trade.

Container ships are categorised according to "generation". The first generation containerships were converted general purpose vessels, the second generation were the first purpose built ships built for the carriage of containers. The third generations were ships built to maximum dimensions allowing their passage through the locks of the Panama Canal. The fourth generation containership has a breadth greater than the width of the Panama Canal which restricts its ability to move between the Atlantic and Ocean Basins. They are also known as post-panamax containerships. The development of the post-panamax containership has allowed the expansion of container carrying capacity and the term Very Large Container Ship (VLCS) to be used. Feeder Container Ships refer to container ships which are employed to move containers from regional ports to hub port.

Figure 2.17 – Post-panamax Cellular Container Ship "Emma Maersk"
The world's largest container ship (2006) with a capacity exceeding 11,000 TEU

Figure 2.18 – Fully 'geared' Heavy Lift Ship

(Photo: Jumboship)

The container ship has many features of design interest, including large hatchways, with a width corresponding to the width of the cargo holds (in excess of 80% the width of the ship), single holds fitted with cellular guides for under deck stowage of containers, strong hatch covers designed to bear the weight of tiers of containers carried on deck and a hull structure which compensates for shear forces, bending moments and torsion. The majority of the 3,700 cellular container ships engaged on liner routes between developed nations are gearless and depend on shore equipment for load and discharge operations. The size of a container ship is normally measured by the number of standard 20 foot containers it can carry. The first purpose built deep – sea container ships were capable of carrying 1,500 20 foot equivalent units (TEU) Presently there are designs for Very Large Container Carriers (VLCS) able to carry in excess of 13,500 TEU. The largest cellular container ship presently in operation (2006) is the "Emma Maersk" which has a capacity reported by its owners in excess of 11,000 TEU. In addition to containerships engaged on international main line routes container ships have been designed for the distribution of containers between hub and feeder ports. These are known as feeder container ships which vary in size from 150TEU to 2,000TEU depending on service demand.

2.16   ROLL ON – ROLL OFF SHIPS

The Roll On – Roll Off (RO RO) concept developed alongside containerisation and at one time was considered to be a realistic alternative. RO RO ships are designed to accommodate vehicles which can be driven on or off specially designed garage decks through watertight doors at the end or sides of the ship.

There are about 5,000 RO RO ships in service (2006) which include the following subcategories

- RO RO   Most ferries on significant routes have RO RO Capability

- RO PAX   Roll On/Roll Off Passenger (Freight some Passenger accommodation)

- CACA   Car Carrier

- CONT RO Containers Roll On – Roll Off Deep Sea Combined Carrier

Cargoes are presented to the ship either as accompanied tractor trailer combinations or as unit loads requiring stowage by port workers. Access between ship and shore is by use of a ship's ramp. There are three types of ship's ramp, namely: fixed axial ramps, fixed quarter ramps and slewing quarter ramps.

2.17   BARGE CARRIERS

Other ship types used in the carriage of unitised cargoes include the Barge Carrier. The barge system consists of three elements; the mother ship, the barge handling system and the barge. The barges are designed to consolidate break-bulk cargoes and can carry bulk cargoes. They are compatible with ISO freight containers. Barge carriers are used between ports which have a substantive inland waterway hinterland. The best known systems are;

- LASH   Lighter Aboard Ship Barges lifted onboard by stern gantry

- SEABEE   Barges carried onboard and stowed by 'lift and roll' method

- BACAT   Barge Catamaran

2.18   HEAVY LIFT SHIPS

An increasingly important sector for the carriage of indivisible cargoes is the heavy lift ship. Whilst small in numbers the heavy lift sector comprises two main types of ship, those which have Lift On Lift Off (LO LO) heavy lift capability and those which are of the semi-submersible form. Using derrick crane systems the LO LO can lift single cargoes which weigh up to 2500 tonnes, mass. The semi-submersible heavy lift ship is less flexible, but can carry indivisible cargoes of many times the weight of the LO LO heavy lift ship. Semi-submersible lifts include the carriage of oil rig platforms.

2.19   PASSENGER SHIPS

The carriage of passengers by sea is an important and growing activity. The two most important categories of passenger ship are the ferry and the cruise ship. The traditional passenger liner, (a passenger ship engaged on a regular timetabled route) is extinct with the exception of the trans-Atlantic liner service provided by the 'Queen Mary 2'.

Ferry

The ferry is a ship built to provide a floating bridge across a relatively narrow waterway. The maximum recognised length of a ferry route is 24 hours. Great innovation in ferry development aimed at meeting or creating market demand has been seen over past years. Structures include the conventional mono hull ferry and the high speed ferry with catamaran or trimaran wave piercing hull form. The use of "Wing In Ground" (WIG) technology is a future possibility to develop very high speed ferries which 'skim' across the sea.

Cruise Ship

Cruising has become established as a leisure activity for many to meet the demand there are more than 430 dedicated cruise ships in world service. In addition there are a small number of general purpose and container ships which provide accommodation for the world traveller. Cruise ships are designed for specific markets. The cruise ship can be categorised by the number of passengers it carries or its size in gross tonnage:

Passenger Numbers	Gross Tonnage	Category
Up to 500	2,000 gt – 24,999 gt	Small
500 – 1,000	25,000 gt – 49,000 gt	Mid
Over 1,000	50,000 gt – 20,000 gt	Large

Figure 2.19 – Passenger Liner/Cruise Ship: 'Queen Mary 2'

(Photo: BBC News)

Figure 2.20 – RO PAX Ferry 'Stena Britannica'

(Photo: P. Wright)

An alternative category is established by facilities, including standard of accommodation and service quality offered to the passenger. The following sub-categories are used:

- Luxury Cruise ship

- Premier Cruise ship

- Standard Cruise ship

The features of a cruise ship include passenger cabins, public spaces and recreation areas. Presently the largest cruise ships can carry 3000 passengers and a crew of 1500 persons and there are plans to make them capable of carrying 5,000 passengers. Cruise ships operate from home port with ports of call built into the cruise itinerary. Whilst self-contained when at sea, the cruise ship demand on a home port and its infrastructure for an efficient turnaround is considerable.

2.20   ALL OTHER TYPES OF SHIPS

A wide variety of non cargo carrying ships may be of interest to the port manager and will either be employed or supported by the port. Other ship types using a port may include fishing vessels, warships and vessels associated with the offshore industry. Ships used by port authorities will include pilot boats, dredgers, salvage vessels, lighthouse/buoy tenders, tugs and hydrographic survey vessels.

2.21 SELF-ASSESSMENT AND TEST QUESTIONS

Attempt the following and check your answers from the text.

1. Where can you find information about (i) the size of the world fleet and (ii) details of contemporary ship design?

2. State the purpose of designating a load line to a ship and describe its impact on the ship's commercial operation.

3. List the commercial and physical concerns which are considered in evaluating basic ship particulars, prior to detailed design.

4. What is meant by the term "general cargo"?

5. State four methods of consolidating general cargo and comment on the effectiveness of each method on port operations.

6. Discuss the meaning of the following terms which refer to the characteristics of bulk cargoes: (i) flammability (ii) friability (iii) abrasiveness (iv) thixotropicity (v) toxicity (vi) corrositivity.

Using the information provided in the Distance and Time Table Figure 2.11 establish the distance covered on one leg of a container "pendulum" route between London (Thamesport) and Vancouver using the Suez Canal.

7. If the Suez Canal were closed and the ship were routed via the Cape of Good Hope what would be the **difference in distance**?

8. What would be the **difference in time** on the same pendulum route between a passage using the Suez Canal or Cape of Good Hope?

Assume the container ship averaged 22 knots on passage, the total Suez Canal transit took 24 hours and six days were allocated for loading and unloading **at each end** of the "pendulum" route.

9. What are the fundamental differences in design between a crude oil tanker and a tanker designed to carry chemical cargoes?

10. State the feature of iron ore carrier design which helps to reduce structural stress and improve stability.

11. What are the meaning of the following terms related to container ships: (i) TEU. (ii) FEU. (iii) LCL. (iv) Slot. (v) Hold. (vi) Bay.

Having completed Chapter Two attempt **ONE** of the following and submit your essay to your Tutor.

1. Choose any **TWO** of the following ship types and discuss the main features of design. For each type chosen draw a simple transverse (cross) section. Label the significant structural parts.

   (a) Cellular container ship

   (b) Very large crude oil carrier

   (c) Iron ore carrier

   (d) General purpose ship

OR

2. Describe the market and pattern of international seaborne trade, for any **TWO** bulk cargoes with which you are familiar. Comment on the risk factors associated with transport by sea.

Chapter 3

PORT MANAGEMENT

3.1   INTRODUCTION

The European Sea Ports Organisation (ESPO) defines the port as *'an area of land and water including facilities, destined mainly for receiving vessels, loading, unloading and storing cargoes, receiving and delivering the cargoes to land transport means'*. They may also include activities of firms linked to the sea-borne trade.

The facilities associated with the port including entry and departure of ships and the use of loading/unloading facilities need to be managed.

Chapter Three looks at the rationale, functions, organisational structure and management responsibilities. Ports are expensive and operate in a highly competitive market. Management needs to be informed of the standards of performance achieved. Safety and security within a port is critical to the reputation of a port and these are briefly considered. Finally the Chapter will consider the role of Statutory Bodies such as Customs, Immigration and Port Health, and the needs of port users.

3.2   RATIONALE OF THE PORT BUSINESS

For several reasons, there is always a need to move goods from one place to another, and sometimes through water and sea transportation. The demand for maritime transport is justified by the need to trade, and therefore maritime transport is usually treated as a "driven demand". This demand has increased significantly in the last two decades with the old logic of trade stemming from the concept of 'absolute and comparative advantages' being overtaken by recent economic and trade developments such as globalisation, free trade agreements and improvements in packaging and transport technology. The concept includes containerisation and unitisation of cargo packaging, increase of ships' size and speed, intermodal and logistical developments, advances in electronic commerce and information technology.

As much of sea transportation is performed internationally, shipping or maritime business can be regarded as a service sector entirely dependent on the demand and supply of world trade. In this approach, the port activity is considered as a sub-sector of the maritime industry, with its main role being restricted to the provision of services to both ships and cargoes, and facilitation of the movement of goods and passengers between land and sea. A port manager, whose job is to satisfy the needs of different port customers and users (shippers, shipowners, agents and intermediaries), is therefore required to understand the reasons and mechanisms of trade, and how his/her own port can benefit or lose from the changes in world sea-borne trade, and the variations in the patterns of maritime and intermodal transportation.

Another way to look at maritime business in general, and at ports in particular, is to consider freight transport (or the transport of goods) as an integrated part of the logistics system. The basis of logistics is the integration and optimisation of different functions and processes for the purpose of overall cost reduction and customer satisfaction. Unlike the economic and trade approach the logistics approach integrates transport with other components such as purchasing, production, storage, inventory management, and marketing. In this approach, ports are seen as "logistics and distribution centres" that optimise the movement of goods and services within the entire transport and logistics chain and provide an opportunity to add value to the goods. Value can be added by offering services such as assembly of components, repacking, labelling, quality control and just in time distribution. The role of ports as logistics centres has been fully recognised in recent years. It is not surprising to find that the most efficient and well-managed ports in the world are those providing first-class 'logistics and value added services'. The port manager needs therefore to understand the different aspects of logistics management, how to properly apply and implement them within a port context.

Ports as a major component of the maritime industry have an important role to play in world trade, international logistics and global supply chains. Port manager's need to understand and be aware of the two main dimensions of modern seaports; ports as trade gateways and corridors and ports as logistics and distribution centres.

3.3   PORT FUNCTIONS

Figure 3.1 below illustrates the port functions and how the various activities are synchronised from the arrival of the ship up to its departure.

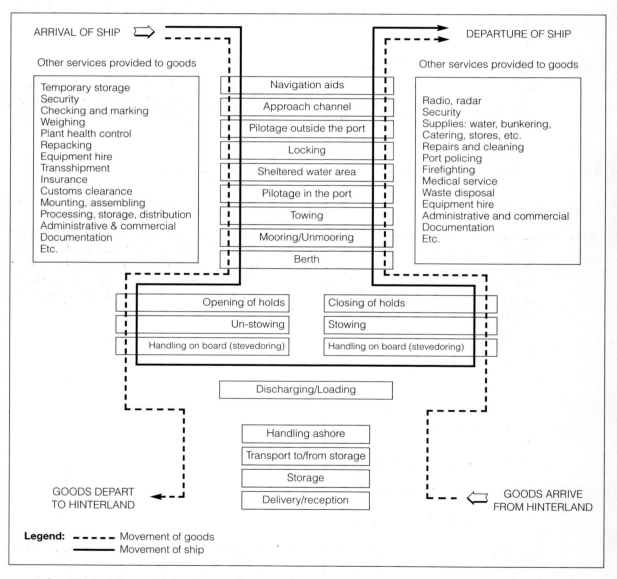

Figure 3.1 – Main Operational and Administrative Functions of a Port

(Source: UNCTAD)

Port functions and activities are typically broken down into services to ships and services to cargo, but this classification does neither reflect the complex portfolio of port services, nor include the different landside and intermodal operations of modern ports. A better way to analyse port functions is to look at the way different services are structured throughout the various port assets and facilities as shown below in Figure 3.2.

Nautical Infrastructure (Sea or water connection)	Berth or quay infrastructure (Shore interface)	Port superstructure (Land-side & intermodal extension)
Marine Services – Conservancy & protection – Access & navigation – Pilotage and towage – Vessel traffic management – Dredging & maintenance	**Terminal Services** – Berthing – Tie-up services – Stevedoring and wharf handling – Bunkering and supply – Quay transfer operations	**Logistics & Value Added Services** – Cargo storage & processing – Information processing – Estate and rental services – Repair services – Other logistics & value added services

Figure 3.2 – Breakdown of Port Functions by Type of Assets and Facilities

3.4   PORT ORGANISATION

Ports regularly wonder about the consistency between their purposes (or missions) and the fulfilment of their assignments. Apart from the general assignment as a common public authority, the mission of any port lies within one or a combination of the following:

1.   A land property owner, trader or developer

2.   An investor in either infrastructure, superstructure, or both

3.   An operator, manager and provider of part or all of services to ships and cargo

Historically, ports were both owned and managed by public entities, mainly through port authorities, who performed most functions including navigation, infrastructure, superstructure development, ship and cargo operations and management. The present strong trend towards privatisation ensures that the organisation of most world ports lies somewhere between purely private ports and totally public ports. Typically, one or a variation of the following types of organisation would be involved in port management;

- Private company,

- Semi-public company,

- Public enterprise,

- Public establishment,

- Municipal or regional authority,

- Port national office,

- Public administration

From the different objectives of the organisations associated with port management, four ports' models have emerged; service ports, landlord ports, tool ports, and private ports. Each have different degrees of ownership and commitment to the management of ship and cargo operations including the employment and control of the labour force.

	Infrastructure	Superstructure	Workforce
Landlord	YES	NO	NO
Tool	YES	YES	NO
Service	YES	YES	YES
Private	ALL TOTALLY OWNED AND OPERATED BY THE PRIVATE SECTOR		

Figure 3.3 – Main ports' organisational status

There is no standard model that accommodates the various organisational status of world ports. One of the main reasons behind this is that whilst sea transport has developed internationally, the development of the port sector has taken place usually at the local or national level. Another reason is the definition and the extent of which the role the public authority is determined. The presence of the public authority in ports is usually evidenced by the presence of statutory bodies which supervise maritime activities (e.g. coast guards, Vessel Traffic Services (VTS) and marine safety services), or ensure the compliance with national and international regulations of ships calling at the port, and goods and passengers passing through it (port state control, customs clearance and health control), Apart from the functions carried out by the public power, other port activities can be carried out by commercial operators. Industrial investment can be undertaken either by the public or private sector.

	Description	Strengths	Weaknesses
Landlord Port	• Owns, develops and maintains the infrastructure, but leases it to the private sector	• Private firms to handle cargo with their own equipment • Investments by the private sector ensure strong market leadership, long-term relationship	• Power and sometimes conflict between private sector ambitions and general public interest • Over capacity • Possible footloose operations
Tool Port	• Owns, develops and maintains the infrastructure • Owns, operates the superstructure (shore cranes, sheds & warehouses) • Handling operations and other marine services performed by private sector	• Huge investment by the public authority • No redundancy (in theory)	• Double entity (public and private) undertaking cargo operations and management • Possibility of conflict regarding equipment's assignment and operational efficiency
Service Port	• Owns, maintains, and develops both infrastructure and superstructure • Owns, operates handling equipment • Operates on its own all port functions & the services to customers	• Unity of command and management	• Handling operations not compatible with administrative duties • Private sector out of the port business • Strong power from trade unions
Private Port	• Everything is owned and operated by the private sector, apart from regulatory and statutory functions which are performed by the public authority	• Management less influenced by political decisions • Higher efficiency in asset and human resources management (in theory)	• Risk of monopoly • Possible deviation from core business to more profitable activities • Risk of footloose arrangements (private sector leaving the port)

Figure 3.4 – Description, Strengths and Weaknesses of Different Port Organisational Models

As with port functions, the organisation of port services varies greatly by time and space, and sometimes it may take decades to change a port's organisation from one status to another, since institutional and legal constraints may constitute a barrier to reform. There is no 'perfect' model port in terms of operational efficiency, service quality, and profit earnings. Within each of the four typical port models, activities need to be organised to interface smoothly with one another, and ultimately ensure maximum efficiency and better quality at a reasonable cost to port customers and users. Good organisation, management, and collaboration among the various port operators help improve the overall service to the customer.

3.5 PORT ORGANISATIONAL STRUCTURE

A typical port will have common functional elements regardless of the structural model. The elements consist of the Board of Directors, Marine, Traffic, Management Services, Finance and Engineering. A Port Advisory Group may be established to advise the Board of Directors on issues concerning practical operational problems and potential developments.

Marine functional staff include the Harbourmaster, pilots, port craft operative and Vessel Traffic Systems (VTS) operators. The areas of responsibility include the maintenance of channels and navigation aids, the movement of ships and use of port craft (pilot cutters, hydrographic survey launches), the management of pilots and those involved in VTS, and the collection of marine statistics. **Traffic functions** concern shore based activities and involves aspects of cargo handling, berth allocation, supervision of work and control of cargo entry to the port and port terminals. Port **Management Services** fulfil the following functions, the provision of information, public relations and port promotion, market research and port planning. Persons skilled in economics, engineering, operational research and cargo handling systems will be members of the **Port Advisory Group**.

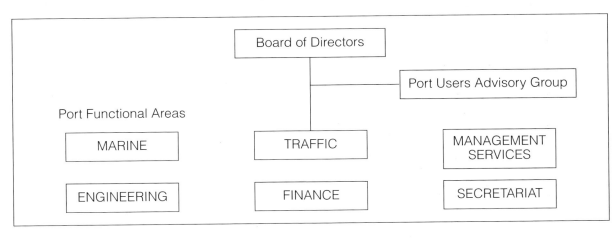

Figure 3.5 – Typical Port Organisational Structure

A port is a financial entity with large flows of income and expenditure which need to be controlled and managed. The **finance** function is to control and prepare budgets, collect revenues, make payments, prepare accounting statements and provide financial statistics. A port also requires **engineering** skills to undertake the maintenance and development of the fabric of the port structure in areas such as civil engineering, mechanical, marine and electrical works. Engineers also provide necessary expertise for port planning. A Secretariat is involved in the port organisation and covers functions which include legal and human resource advice, liaison between functional groups, port security, public correspondence and general administration.

3.6   PORT PERFORMANCE MEASUREMENT

An indication of port performance is important and will become increasingly so as ship size continues to grow, competition increases and capital intensity of port investment rises. Features concerning port productivity include: vessel turnaround time, cargo volume handled and speed of cargo handling. A further measure of port productivity may concern cargo safety and pilferage prevention.

Performance indicators are control tools or instruments that allow port managers to measure port or terminal performance, and take corrective decisions to improve it when and where it is needed. They are also useful for investment decision strategies, and for port planning and forecasting. Ports are a major cost element of the maritime and intermodal transport chain. According to studies, two thirds of the total maritime costs take place in ports, during wharfage, handling and storage operations. Port costs include port dues and costs invoiced by agents for various port operations. The cost of ships time and quality of service is not ignored. The port manager has to resourcefully manage the many different operations within the port to reach an optimal service level, where waste and delay is kept to the minimum. He also has to prepare for future operations through good forecasting and planning. There will be no smooth operations without good planning. The next section of Chapter Three will focus on the measurement and optimisation of **port operations**. Issues relating to port planning and forecasting will be discussed in Chapter Five. It is helpful to read this Section along with Chapter Five to fully understand the different concepts and techniques related to port performance measurement.

Port operations performance can be considered under **three** broad categories:

1.   **Physical performance** refers to the output of existing assets and facilities. The performances of the port can be calculated as a whole, or the performances for each set or group of facilities (berths, yards, cranes, sheds, storehouses and labour force), can be considered.

2.   **Quality performance** is a factor of competition which may exceed the price of port services in importance. Port reliability, flexibility and application of rules are all included in the quality of port services.

3.   **Financial performance** is described as the profit and loss contribution of each category of port operation and service.

Performance indicators need to be established in a quantifiable manner to allow objective analysis and comparison. Vigilance should be used when comparing port performances because indicators are not always calculated or interpreted in the same way. For example when considering container terminal handling performance, throughput measurements do not specify container status (eg FCL, LCL, empty containers). Good performance indicators require reliable data as well as a detailed description of the meaning for the use of each indicator.

The following sections looks at the performance indicators used in four key areas of port operations namely berth performance indicators, handling operation indicators, storage operation indicators and quality of service indicators.

3.7   BERTH PERFORMANCE INDICATORS

Berth performance indicators essentially concern the calculation of ship's waiting time and its time in port. A problem for port managers is to ensure optimum use of berths in the port. Insufficient berth capacity will result in delays to the ship, excess capacity will be a wasted use of port capital and resource. The main indicators used to assess berth performance are:

- Berth Throughput

- Waiting Time

- Service Time

- Time in Port

- Grade of Waiting

- Berth Occupancy Ratio

- Berth Working Time Ratio

Berth Throughput The berth throughput indicator is the total tonnage or number of units handled on one berth in a given period of time (weeks, months or years). Berth throughput is a measure of berth activity. Units of berth throughput include, TEU throughput at container berths, tonnes moved at bulk and general cargo berths and number of vehicles handled at RO-RO berths. Some port operations, such as transhipment and re-stowage, involve double handling and double counting.

Berth Throughput (BT) = Total units handled in a period of time

Waiting Time is defined as the time a ship spends waiting for an available berth that is, the delay between a ship's arrival in the port and its tying up at the berth. A performance indicator used by port management is the **Waiting Ratio** which for an individual ship can be established by the formula:

$$\text{Waiting Ratio} \quad = \quad \frac{\text{Time waiting for a berth}}{\text{Service Time}}$$

Service Time is defined as the time a ship stays at a berth whether it is working or not. The service time is established from first line ashore to the time the last line is let go. A performance indicator, the **Service Time Ratio** can be established for a berth, terminal or port using the formula

$$\text{Service Time Ratio} \quad = \quad \frac{\text{Cumulated Service Time}}{\text{Total Number of Ships}}$$

Time in Port or **Turnaround time** is the total time the ship spends in the port from arrival at the port to final departure. A performance indicator, Time in Port ratio can be established for a berth terminal or port using the formula

$$\text{Time in Port Ratio} \quad = \quad \frac{\text{Cumulated Waiting Time} + \text{Service Time}}{\text{Total number of ships}}$$

Grade of Waiting For commercial reasons it is very frequent to calculate a Grade of Waiting (GW) ratio. The comparison of the waiting time with the service time provides a good indicator of what is acceptable by **shipowners**. Shipowners usually accept a 10% Grade of Waiting ratio beyond which the port is considered as inefficient or of low quality.

$$\text{Grade of Waiting Ratio} \quad = \quad \frac{\text{Cumulated Waiting Time}}{\text{Cumulated Service Time}}$$

Berth Occupancy Ratio is the ratio determined by dividing the time a berth has been occupied (in hours per year) by the total number of hours in a year (8760). It shows the level of demand for port services.

$$\text{Berth Occupancy Ratio} \quad = \quad \frac{\text{Total Service Time (per berth)}}{\text{Hours in a Year (8760)}}$$

Berth Working Time Ratio is a ratio which relates the number of hours during which a ship is worked in port during the Total Service time on the berth. It informs whether or not there is a long idle time during berth operations. For example, a berth working time ratio of 50% means that the port works only 12 hours a day and the ship is idle for 12 hours.

$$\textbf{Berth Working Time Ratio} \quad = \quad \frac{\text{Total Time Worked}}{\text{Total Service Time}}$$

3.8 HANDLING OPERATION INDICATORS

When assessing berth performance only the port or berth infrastructure is concerned. In handling operations three sets of resources are considered namely Ship/Shore Handling Equipment, Yard Transfer Equipment and the Labour Force. The indicators below are frequently used for the measurement of the performance of the handling operations. Because of peak situations it is preferable to calculate the ratios on a monthly or a daily basis, as the yearly average does not show the periods when the problems happen.

Ship Output indicators measure the rate at which the cargo is handled to and from a vessel. There are three ship output indicators namely; working ship output, berth ship output and port ship output:

$$\textbf{Working Ship Output} \quad = \quad \frac{\text{Total tonnage handled}}{\text{Total hours worked}} \quad \textit{(tonnes /ship hour worked)}$$

$$\textbf{Berth Ship Output} \quad = \quad \frac{\text{Total tonnage handled}}{\text{Total hours on the berth}} \quad \textit{(tonnes /ship hour on berth)}$$

$$\textbf{Port Ship Output} \quad = \quad \frac{\text{Total tonnage handled}}{\text{Total hours in port}} \quad \textit{(tonnes/ship hour in port)}$$

Gang Output The ship output depends among others, on the number and efficiency of gangs used for handling. Except in small old fashioned ports, the gang includes not only workers but also the handling equipment for ship to shore operations and quay transfer operations. It follows that gang output varies by type and capacity of the equipment used, the cargo type and onboard position of cargo. In some ports, the average output is calculated per man x hour. The following Gang Output indicators are used:

$$\textbf{Average Output/Gang/Hour} \quad = \quad \frac{\text{Tonnage handled}}{\text{Total gang X hours worked}}$$

$$\textbf{Average Number of Gangs/Ship} \quad = \quad \frac{\text{Total number of gangs}}{\text{Number of ships}}$$

Utilisation Ratios refer to the effectiveness of resource utilisation and include both machinery and the human resource:

$$\textbf{Rate of Utilisation of Cranes} \quad = \quad \frac{\text{Number of worked hours}}{\text{Number of available hours}}$$

$$\textbf{Rate of Utilisation of Workers} \quad = \quad \frac{\text{Number of man hours worked}}{\text{Number of man hours available}}$$

('available' time refers to the time a machine or resource is available for use, less periods for maintenance and bad weather).

3.9   STORAGE OPERATION INDICATORS

Most ports of the world have to provide covered transit warehouses for break-bulk cargo, container freight stations for Less than Container Load (LCL) cargoes, tanks for liquid bulk storage yards for open storage, space and warehouses for long term storage, The facilities have costs for initial capital outlay, maintenance and operations. Space requirements for shed and open storage capacity are always difficult to determine because of the different characteristics of cargoes presented. and the time cargo will dwell in storage. The port's commercial strategy will also determine the amount of transit space required. If transit space is readily available the port will attempt to attract cargo by offering a low tariff on storage. Alternatively if transit space is limited or expensive the port will impose extra dues on storage to speed up delivery times and reduce time in transit.

Dwell Time is the time spent by a cargo in port and usually refers to containers. It can be applied to other cargo types.

Average Dwell Time is a utilisation ratio which does not concern port layout, capacity, and space requirements. The formula for establishing the average dwell time is valid for both open and covered storage.

$$\textbf{Average Dwell Time} \quad = \quad \frac{\text{Tonnage x dwell time}}{\text{Total tonnage stored per day}}$$

3.10   QUALITY OF SERVICE INDICATORS

The quality of port services is a major requirement of both ship and cargo interests. The waiting ratio and dwell time ratio are two of the many ratios which can be used as quality of service indicators. Shippers and shipowners are also concerned by a port's adherence to quality assurance programmes such as the International Standard Organisations (ISO) 9000 Quality Management standards and the ISO 14000 Environmental Management standards. Social working conditions for port employees are also indicators of service quality. The following ratios are samples of quality service indicators used by ports:

Working Hours Indicator The co-ordination of all administrative and operational services is one of the key features of port efficiency. The target is to reach a simultaneous working schedule for all services and departments.

$$\textbf{Working Hours Ratio} \quad = \quad \frac{\text{Number of non-coordinated hours}}{\text{24 hours}}$$

The following example illustrates a typical situation where various institutional departments within the port community do not co-ordinate their working hours:

Service	Opening hours	Non-coordinated hours
Tugs/Pilots	0600 – 2200	8 hours
Handling	0000 – 2400	0 hours
Customs clearance	0800 – 1800	14 hours
Delivery/receipt	0600 – 2000	10 hours
Port office	0700 – 1700	14 hours
Total non coordinated hours		**46 hours**

Figure 3.6 – Working Hours Non-Coordinated

Answer: **Working Hour Ratio** $= \dfrac{46}{24} =$ **1:1.92**

Punctuality Ratio refers to the port's ability to respect the forecasted times and schedules as planned. The ratio is the difference between planned and actual arrival and departure times and the number of ship calls made.

$$\textbf{Punctuality Ratio} \quad = \quad \frac{\text{Total delayed time}}{\text{Number of ship calls}}$$

Reliability Ratio A perfectly reliable port is the one where there is no disruptive events that could undermine the scheduled work.

$$\textbf{Reliability Ratio} \quad = \quad \frac{\text{Number of effective days worked}}{\text{Number of scheduled working days}}$$

3.11 CONTAINER TERMINAL PERFORMANCE

As container operations are becoming more prominent, their measurement of performance is briefly considered. The traditional method of establishing container terminal efficiency is the average number of container moves handled (loaded/discharged) by the quayside gantry crane per hour. Across the container ports industry the figure can range between 10 and 50 container moves /hour/gantry.

Other Productivity measures, shown below as annual figures, give a broad appreciation of container terminal performance on an annual basis by UK ports. For operational purposes they could be provided on a more frequent basis.

Productivity Measurement	Annual achievable productivity (UK 2005)
TEU/Metre berth	1,100
TEU/Hectare	21,500
TEU/Gantry	120,000

Figure 3.7 – Container terminal productivity measurement

(Source: Cardiff University)

3.12 NATURE OF MARINE OPERATIONS

Port Marine Operations consists of ensuring the safety of the ship from arrival at the port limits to its final departure. The Harbourmaster is the person who has responsibility for port activities and is able to exercise jurisdiction to ensure the safety of the port and port users, the sustainability of the port environment and emergency preparedness. The Port Authority, through the Harbourmaster, is responsible for navigation which includes the provision of navigation aids, the survey and maintenance of channels, the appointment of pilots and the provision of Vessel Traffic Services.

Navigation aids within a port include buoys, fixed beacons, leading lights and traffic signals. Navigation aids are costly items to purchase and maintain and their purpose needs to be established before installation.

Hydrographic surveys of the port area are undertaken to confirm the depth of water in the channels, the positioning of navigation aids and provide information regarding tidal heights and streams.

Dredging in port areas is undertaken for different purposes including the maintenance of channel depth, capital dredging, deepening of channels to take deeper drafted ships or specialist dredging required for civil engineering works. Dredging is an expensive operation which is only undertaken when necessary, which may mean continuously for river ports. There are two distinct types of dredgers mechanical dredgers, which include the bucket dredger, and hydraulic dredgers which include the trailing suction dredger. Disposal of dredged spoil is a serious problem and can be put to beneficial use, e.g. land reclamation, or disposed of in either open water or confined structures to limits imposed by licenses. Confined structures are used when dredged material containing contaminated solids is to be separated from the water in which it is carried. The environmental effects of dredging may impact upon water quality and natural habitats. Dredging may cause changes to both physical processes and underwater topography.

Pilots are mariners who have local knowledge and provide advise to the Masters of ships entering and leaving port. In the United Kingdom, responsibility for the provision of pilotage services rests with a competent harbour authority. The competent harbour authority has the power to determine the qualifications required and authorise persons to act as pilots. They also make pilotage direction specifying the types and size of ships which are subject to compulsory pilotage and the areas where pilotage acts must take place. After examination it may be possible for Masters of regular traders to be issued with a Pilotage Exemption Certificate.

Vessel Traffic Services (VTS) are designed to enhance and improve the safety of ships within port areas. The International definition of a VTS is *"a service implemented by a competent authority designed to improve the safety and efficiency of vessel traffic and to protect the environment. The service shall have the capability to interact with marine traffic and respond to traffic situations developing in the VTS area"*. The Vessel Traffic Service will be either active or passive. An active VTS will act as a traffic control tool through which port traffic will be organised and regulated. A passive VTS system provides information regarding traffic movements and other matters of interest to port users and is advisory. In major ports the role of VTS is indispensable and allows for a 24 hour seven day a week port operation to be maintained irrespective of visibility and other weather conditions. Information of ships carrying dangerous cargoes is of particular importance for port safety. The main components of a VTS system are a building for control operatives, a radar tracking system, a communications system and data handling capability.

3.13 NATURE OF CARGO OPERATIONS

Cargo operations concern the loading and discharge of a ship. There are three principles which are considered namely:

1. Safety of crew and persons onboard
2. Safety of the ship
3. Safety of the cargo

Cargo operations have to be expedited in the most efficient manner possible. The Shipowner will be concerned to minimise port time as a ship is only making money when it is functioning as a transport vehicle. The role of the ship's Officer in port is to maintain a watch and supervise all activities onboard the ship, including the loading and discharge of cargo, the monitoring of the ship's stability and ensuring the ship's security and safety. The ship's Officer needs to be fully aware of the safety legislation and regulations which concern the ship in port. Ship and shore personnel are required by law to fully liaise in the loading and discharge of the ship. This is particularly the case for specific ship types, namely bulk carriers and tankers where a Ship Shore Safety Check-list will be completed prior to the load and discharge operation. The Code of Practice for the Safe Loading of Bulk Carriers, (the BLU Code) also places responsibility on both parties to ensure that the load and discharge operation is conducted in accordance with the plan agreed by both parties before commencement of operations.

3.14 PORT SAFETY MANAGEMENT

Port Safety in the United Kingdom is subject to the Health and Safety at Work Act (1974) and regulated through the Dock Regulations (1988) and the Dangerous Goods in Harbours Regulations (1987). The Port Marine Safety Code (2003) gives advice concerning safe marine operations in ports. The development of a Quality Management System through **ISO 9002** recognises the need for safety management. Combined with the implementation of the International Safety Management Code for the Safe Operation of Ships and Pollution Prevention (**ISM Code**) the management of safety in ports is well developed.

3.15 PORT SECURITY

Port Security is an issue which due to the recent upsurge in terrorist activity has been much in focus. Terrorism is only one security concern which ports have to consider. Others concerns include, smuggling, stowaways, asylum seekers, illegal immigrants, sabotage, theft and pilferage of cargo.

	ISM Code	ISO 9002 Series	ISPS Code
Aim	Safety of Ships and pollution prevention	Quality assurance of products and services	Security of maritime network, and prevention of terrorism threats
Target	Marine mgt. and shipboard operation	Contractual relationship between customer/supplier	Ship, port and mobile off-shore facilities, ship/port operations and mgt.
Completion	Capacity to meet safety & pollution prevention	Demonstrate ability of marine management and shipboard operation to meet customer requirements	Ability of participants to meet security requirements, and react to changing security levels
Means	Implementation of the safe operation of ships & pollution prevention	Implementation of a quality assurance system	Implementation of part A of the code & chapter x1-2 of SOLAS. Regional implementation of part B
Scheme of certification	Company assessment: doc. of compliance Ship assessment: safety mgt. certificate	Company and ships assessment: Quality system certificate	ISSC, SSA and SSP for ships & companies. Local accreditation of PFPA & PFSP for ports
Management of certification	Follow-up assessment each year, re-assessment after 3 years	Surveillance on company every 6 months, all ships during 3 years. Re-assessment after 3 years	Up to 5 years for ISSC & intermediate verifications. Period of validity for the statement of compliance of PFSP to be decided by contracting government

Figure 3.8 – Relationship Between the ISPS Code and Other Safety/Quality Management Programmes

Enhancement of security measures to combat one activity implies improved general security. Security measures in port areas include adequate lighting, strongly constructed security fencing, good warehouse design, strict control on entry and exit gates, identification of port users, appropriate take up of security guard references and training. The recent IMO, International Ship and Port Facility Security Code (ISPS Code) referred to in Chapter Five, links port security activities with those of the ship. Safety and Security concerns are related as is shown in Figure 3.8 above.

3.16 STATUTORY BODIES

The port provides an entry and exit point to a nation state. Certain statutory bodies have an interest in being present in order to ensure the demands of society are met. The three most important are Customs, Immigration and Port Health

Customs. The role of Customs is to ensure control is exercised over the export and import of goods moving across its national borders. Customs also maintain a statistical record of the nations exports and imports allowing governmental assessment of the nation's balance of payments. All ships are required to report to Customs prior to entry and request clearance before departure. On entry into a port the following must be declared. general information about the ship, its voyage and details of ships stores. The ship's Master and each crew member must declare certain goods, for example the number of cigarettes in their possession, A declaration of cargo carried is required and this can be undertaken by submitting the ship's manifest or using a computerised inventory control system approved by Customs. A separate crew and passenger list must be provided to the Customs on entry as well as a listing of crew members and passengers who are leaving the ship at the port. Customs authorities will support the **Marine Safety Agency** and Port Control Inspectorate by sighting Ships Safety Certificates.

Immigration Control is exercised by the Immigration Department of the Government. The purpose of the Department is to prevent illegal immigration and they will need to know crew and passenger names before permitting leave to enter the country. Problems can arise when a crew member or passenger has to be landed for medical reasons, when a crew member deserts the ship, and when a ship arrives in port with shipwrecked seamen onboard. Stowaways are treated as illegal immigrants and dealing with them is the prerogative of the country where arrival takes place.

The World Health Organisation provides regulations which are concerned with preventing the international spread of infectious disease. **Port Health** control is exercised at the ship's arrival and port of departure. Prior to entry the ship's Master is required to declare any case of infectious disease which has occurred. The Port Health Authority may require the ship to anchor in a safe or convenient place in order for a medical inspection to take place and before free pratique (permission to commence port operations and disembarkation of ships personnel) is given. Crew members have to carry valid International Vaccination Certificates. Radio permission may be given to ships entering from a foreign port if the Port Health officer is satisfied that entry of the ship will not result or contribute to the spread of disease. For effective port operation the **flow of standard information** is simplified using community computer networks. The interchange of container information between container terminals for ship planning purposes provides ship and port planners with faster and more accurate data prior to ship arrival. The tracking of containers by various players in the logistics chain allows delivery to be made with greater provision. Computer networks allow for more effective control and clearance of goods through Customs and for the transmission of shipping documents between the shipper, carrier and consignee. The tracking of dangerous goods within and between ports is also essential to ensure correct response in an emergency.

3.17 OTHER PORT USERS

The port is a focal point for many support businesses including ship's Agents, shipping lines and freight forwarders. Increasingly the port is developing businesses which add value to cargoes prior to distribution to the port hinterland.

The **ship's Agent** is appointed by a Shipowner to represent its interests as a local representative. The ship agent's local knowledge will ensure that the activities of the ship are effectively expedited. For the work involved the ship's Agent will receive a fee, in addition to being reimbursed for additional expenses incurred. The activities of the ship's Agent commence before the ships arrival and involve informing and providing specific information to customs, immigration and port health of the expected arrival. The berth will be booked in advance and importer and exporter of cargo will be informed. Tugs and Pilots will be ordered. While in port the ship's Agent will deal with a wide range of activities to support the ship's Master, including crew matters, victuals, spare parts, cargo interests and surveys. On departure of the ship the agent will complete a disbursement account which includes the payment made to the port for dues, tugs and pilots. The disbursement account is submitted to the Shipowner.

A listing of **port users** includes organisations involved with bunker supply, import and export activity, marine engineering, cargo distribution and trucking, chandlery, rigging, cargo and ship survey, towage and salvage, ship repair, terminal operation, mechanical handling equipment, stevedoring, rail freight, warehousing and storage.

Port workers. Ports used to depend on a supply of cheap, mainly unskilled labour for loading and discharging of ships. Technical developments have created a demand for a relatively small, flexible, multi-skilled workforce able to adapt to new technologies and embrace change. In many parts of the developed world the availability of port labour is tight and port organisations have to develop training schemes and resources aimed at young persons with interests in port and related operations. In the United Kingdom, Port Skills and Training Ltd is an organisation which develops and sets the national standard for courses used within the ports and associated industries. The **International Labour Organisation** (ILO) provides training opportunities for port workers involved in container ports through a Port Worker

Development Programme. The programme was established as a result of a report which recognised that the full benefits of ongoing technological progress would not be achieved by developing countries if investment in the port worker was ignored. The programme has more than thirty learning units covering topics ranging from container ship loading operations to the duties of the port supervisor. The Programme is aimed at supervisory grades and below. Port workers are not only facing technological change but also change through the global restructuring of the port authorities and private ports companies. Change presents threats to jobs, pay and conditions and increasing competition can lead to a cut back in the safety of the port worker. Trade unions which represent port workers at a local level respond globally to threats in order to maintain their rights and benefits. More than one hundred and seventy trade unions representing 400,000 port workers are represented by the **International Transport Workers Federation** (ITF) who seeks consultation with port employers to resolve difficulties created by change. The ITF has a specialised Dockers Section which supports port workers in their desire to establish stable and fulfilling employment, decent incomes and working conditions, health and safety in the workplace and the freedom from discrimination and corruption.

3.18   SELF-ASSESSMENT AND TEST QUESTIONS

Attempt the following and check your answers from the text.

1. Discuss why a port activity is described as being 'Demand Driven'?

2. Briefly explain the differences between (i) a Landlord port (ii) a Tool port (iii) a Service port and (iv) a Private port. Give an example of each.

3. List the activities associated with Marine and Engineering functional areas of a port.

4. State the four main activities of a port in which Performance Indicators can be effectively used.

5. What is the value of using Port Performance Indicators to port managers?

6. State the benchmarks which may be used to evaluate a Port Performance Indicator.

7. Expand the abbreviations (i) ISM (ii) ISPS (iii) ISO (iv) VTS (v) PFSP

8. What are the security risks associated with port operations?

9. List the potential impact of port dredging operations on the environment and state how the impact can be reduced.

10. State the various roles of the Customs authority at the port interface.

11. Comment on the challenges and response of port workers faced by a changing ports industry.

12. What is the role of Port State Control in ensuring the quality of merchant ships?

Having completed Chapter Three attempt **ONE** of the following questions and submit your essay to your Tutor.

1. Critically discuss the organisation of port management in meeting the needs of its customers.

OR

2. Explain how operational port performance can be measured. Discuss any weaknesses in the methods you describe.

Chapter 4

PORT FINANCE

4.1 INTRODUCTION

A port is a business and needs to account for the money it receives and the money it spends. In addition a port will need to plan in financial terms for the future. Many of the capital acquisitions made by a port are very long term and intensive in nature. Chapter Four considers the basic principles of finance and accounting. It looks at the need for accounting standards, control and performance measurement. In the latter part of the Chapter economic appraisal and the funding of capital projects is introduced.

4.2 FINANCIAL STATEMENTS AND ACCOUNTING PRINCIPLES

4.2.1 Financial Statements

Financial statements are used to assess the 'financial' performance of firms and organisations. There are three major financial statements, the income statement, the balance sheet, and the statement of cash flows. Usually, the law of a country provides specific rules for preparing financial statements and recording the different costs and revenues.

The **income statement**, also called the profit and loss account, provides information about the operating costs and profits of an organisation over a specific period of time, usually a year. It summarises all the sales and revenues, and any other sources of income, expenses and overheads which take place during that period. The result is a statement that deducts expenses from revenues, and shows whether a firm is making profits or incurring losses.

The **balance sheet** is a statement of a company's financial position at a specific moment in time. It depicts the company's assets and liabilities, in other words what it owns and what it owes. Assets and liabilities are usually put in opposite sides of the balance sheet, but some firms prefer to present them in a vertical form. Assets can be either fixed assets (land, buildings, equipment, vehicles) or current assets, such as cash money, bank deposits and any other items that can easily be turned into cash. Similarly, liabilities are divided into current liabilities (debts for goods and services, accounts payable, overdraft facility and short term loans), long-term debt over several years (loans with a long-term maturity, mortgage, lease), and equity referring to the shareholders' or company owners' money. Therefore in a balance sheet, assets must always equal liabilities plus equity. The balance sheet must not be confused with the *balance of payments* which is a record of debit and credit transactions of a country with foreign countries and international institutions.

The **statement of cash flows** measures the changes in cash over a given period of time. It is similar to the balance sheet, but it registers only cash assets in the left (or upper) side, with remaining assets (depreciation), being registered with the liabilities as deductions.

Depreciation is a very important concept in accounting and financial management. It refers to the amortisation of fixed assets over time, and represents the cost of using owned equipment. For the purpose of tax laws, it is recorded in the financial statements as a cost or expense reflecting a diminishing value of physical asset and equipment. There are different methods to calculate depreciation, but the most commonly used are:

Straight-line depreciation (linear): An equal amount of capital value is allowed every year as a percentage of the original investment. Operating efficiency and repairs remain constant throughout the period. Linear depreciation is used mainly for machinery.

Annual depreciation charge = Original value – Scrap value/Life of asset

Declining balance: Depreciation is highest in the first year and declines year by year with a constant percentage of the remaining book value. Thus the operating efficiency is declining while repairs are increasing. It is often used for vehicles, fixtures and fittings.

Reduced balanced annual depreciation charge = (Remaining) book value x Year %

Annuity: Lowest in the first year and increasing year by year. This is the reverse of the declining balance method and includes the time value of money into the calculation of depreciation. It is only used for property with a long life.

4.3 ACCOUNTING CONTROL AND FINANCIAL PERFORMANCE MEASUREMENT

Financial ratios are useful in monitoring financial results and for strategy formulation. However, they should be interpreted carefully and in line with the port's missions and objectives. In ports, financial ratios should be read together with port physical performance indicators, so as to assess both the overall port efficiency and performance.

Activity

The ratio measures related to the activity measures the financial performances of different operations and activities. Two ratios are often used:

Operating ratio = Operating expenses/ Operating revenues

Operating margin = Operating revenues – Operating expenses/Operating revenues (in %)

Capital Structure

The purpose of this ratio is to measure the relative proportion of the two different types of capital employed in the company, namely Interest'debt and shareholders' equity. The capital structure is usually measured through gearing and leverage ratios. These latter indicate the financial capabilities of a port over a long period of time. A port with a high gearing will be able to pay higher dividends per share than a port with a lower gearing, provided that its return money is higher than the interest rate it pays for the borrowed capital. However, the higher the gearing the greater is the risk to the equity shareholders, and in most cases creditors prefer a low gearing ratio. The ratio of the shareholders' equity is usually called solidity. If the solidity is high it means more of the shareholders' money is tied up in the business but, at the same time, the company is less vulnerable. The main measurement ratios for leverage are:

Gearing Ratio = Interest debt/Equity + Interest debt

Debt service coverage = Gross income/Debt service

Debt -Equity ratio = Total debt/Total equity

Solidity = Equity + reserves/Total balance sheet

Solvency and liquidity

Solvency refers to the ability of a company to pay its debts. Liquidity has a close meaning, and measures the ability of a firm to acquire cash to meet its (immediate) obligations. Solvency is usually expressed in terms of net working capital, while liquidity is often expressed by the Current Ratio:

Current Ratio = Current Assets/Current Liabilities

Net Working Capital = Current Assets – Current Liabilities

Profitability

The profitability of a company is often expressed in terms of one or a combination of two ratios: Return On Equity (ROE), and Return On Assets (ROA).

$$ROE = Net\ profit/Equity$$

$$ROA = Net\ income/Total\ value\ of\ assets$$

4.4   FINANCIAL AND ECONOMIC APPRAISAL OF PORT INVESTMENTS

Private investors by definition seek the commercial profitability of a project, and thus they would typically look at the costs and revenues of a port project, before taking any investment decision. Public authorities, on the other hand, are more concerned with the economic profitability of a port's investment, or, in other words, that they will look at the costs and expected benefits of the project to the port's direct and indirect community, and to the whole economy at large. The assessment and appraisal of port investment therefore varies from case to case. In the first case, investors and their banks usually undertake a financial appraisal of the proposed investment, through analysing the costs of the investment and the generated monetary cash flows, over the project's life span. In the second case, public bodies will primarily undertake a Cost-Benefit Analysis (CBA) and analyse port impacts on the economy. Financial appraisal may also be carried out in the latter case, but it is of a lesser priority.

Modern investment appraisal uses the cash flow approach, where only revenues and expenses related to the investment are taken into consideration, whereas accounting charges, such as depreciation, are not included in the appraisal process. The rationale of the cash flow approach stems from modern finance strategies, which look primarily at the cash generated by an investment so that the revenues accruing from it (including a reasonable profit) will cover the costs and expenses incurred. The basic rule is that only cash-related revenues and expenses will be included in the calculation. For instance, sunk costs referring to the expenses already incurred but not affected by the project, are not included. Similarly, spill-over costs not borne by investors (e.g. pollution, depletion of natural resources) are excluded from calculation.

Another advantage of the approach is the introduction of the discounted rate that looks at the expenses and revenues in the future and at different times so as to account for the effects of risks and inflation. There are two ways to estimate the value of the discount rate. First, through looking at the **opportunity cost of capital**, when for instance government-securities yields 10% per year, and thus every $1 invested today will be worth $1.10 next year, with almost no risk. The second, more widely used, method of estimating the discount rate is to look at the rate of borrowing money from banks, or the **cost of capital**. For instance, if the bank lending rate is 10%, then the value of consuming $1 now is $0.1 (including risk and inflation), since $1.10 needs to be paid next year. Discount rates are published and regularly updated by banks and financial institutions. Three main methods are used in the discounted cash flow approach: namely the pay-back method, the Net Present Value (NPV), and the Internal Rate of Return (IRR).

The Pay-Back method

Payback is the time required for a return on investment. It is the first indicator investors usually use to assess the financial profitability of a project. It is measured by relating the value of the investment to the average annual cash flow.

Pay-Back in years = I/R-C

(Where I = Total investment; R=average annual operating income; C=average annual operating costs)

The Net Present Value (NPV) method

The NPV is the present value of the revenues generated by an investment after minus the capital costs at the time of the investment, and the present value of operating costs. In simple words, the NPV looks at today's value of future money, and is to a large extent the opposite of the interest rate method. An investment is acceptable under the NPV method, when this latter is equal or greater than "0", otherwise it should be rejected. The typical formula to calculate the discount rate is the following:

$$\textbf{NPV (I)} = \sum_{i=n}^{\infty} \frac{1 - (1 + i)^{-n}}{i} * I$$

(Where I = Average annual cash flow or the difference between revenue and costs; n= years and i = discount rate in %)

The Internal Rate of Return (IRR) method

The IRR is the discount rate of equilibrium to the NPV. In other words, it is the discount rate at which the present value of future cash flows equals the cost of the investment. An investment is therefore only acceptable when its IRR exceeds the rate of return.

Simplified Example:

Yearly Costs (C) = 50.000; Yearly Revenues (R) = 90.000; i = 10%; n = 10 years.
NPV (C) = 500.000; NPV (R) = 553.000; NPV = NPV (C) – NPV (R) = 53.000
IRR @ NPV= 0 is 12.4%

The World Bank has modelled the general formula for the NPV and IRR, so as to accommodate the nature and objectives of port projects and long-term investments. For this purpose, the discounted profit is defined as the difference between the discounted investment expenditure and the discounted value of the net benefits generated by the project during its lifetime; and the expression of economic NPV is used to describe it. Thus, for a project whose operations begin in Year n, the discounted profit is calculated as follows:

Year	Yearly Investment	Self or equity financing @ 40% of total	Initial debt	Yearly-debt service @ 10%	Cumulative debt service	Operating expenses	Total Outflow	Expected traffic	Revenue	Net flow
				Millions				Thousands	Millions	
1	2.50	1.00	1.50	0.15	0.15	6.50	8.30	450.00	7.50	**(0.80)**
2	3.45	1.38	2.07	0.21	0.36	6.50	9.13	500.00	9.00	**(0.13)**
3	8.10	3.24	4.86	0.49	0.84	6.50	12.69	530.00	14.00	1.31
4	2.70	1.08	1.62	0.16	1.01	6.50	9.29	600.00	15.00	5.71
5	3.90	1.56	2.34	0.23	1.24	6.50	10.31	620.00	18.00	7.69

(Planned investment spans Self or equity financing and Debt financing (loans) @ 60% of total; Debt financing comprises Initial debt, Yearly-debt service @ 10%, and Cumulative debt service)

Table 4.1 – Example of Financial Appraisal of a Port Project

$$\textbf{NPV Econ} = -C + \sum_{i=n}^{\infty} R /(1 + i)^n$$

Where

n = year in which the infrastructure or project is put in service;

i = national economy discount rate in %;

C = discounted investment cost,

R = Benefit (revenue) in year n

Table 4.1 illustrates an example of how a port investment project is assessed using the cash flow approach. In the example, a port project is to be carried out for 5 years, with yearly investments of 2.5, 3.45, 8.10, 2.7, and 3.9 respectively. 40% of the initial investment is self-financed, whereas the remaining sum is debt-financed with an annual interest rate of 10% on the loan.

4.5 ECONOMIC APPRAISAL OF PORT INVESTMENTS

Since economic appraisal uses a different set of criteria to assess a port's investment, the *definition and assessment* of the revenues and costs are not the same as in the case of the financial method. First, the costs of and benefits from a port's project in the economic appraisal approach are not restricted to the investing body, but are translated to other parties from the port community (eg customers and users) and to the local, regional or national economy. Second, the assessment of revenues and costs is undertaken at different levels when using the financial approach. For instance, taxes are recognised and labour salaries are considered as a social benefit for the community rather than as a cost

The economic appraisal of port investments forms an integral part of the general appraisal of projects in the public sector and thus the concepts of public goods and general interest are of paramount importance. Port impact studies are conducted to decide whether undertaking a port project that will be financed fully or partly by the public sector (national or local governments), or by regional or international institutions such as the EU and the World Bank. Port impact studies not only look at the economic benefits of the project (eg port efficiency, trade benefits and infrastructure developments), but also at its social and environmental impact, e.g. employment, pollution, city extensions. The impact of ports are considered under three headings:

Direct impact: The impact of a port project on the firms and organisations that are directly linked with the port activity, such as the port authority, shippers, shipowners and port operators.

Table 4.2 provides an example of the direct impact of port activities on employment in the port of Le Havre. Similar studies on direct port impacts can be accessed through port's websites, e.g. Ports of Rotterdam and Antwerp

Activities	Performances	Employment needs	Formula used for 100.000 TEU	Year-men needs for 100.000 TEU
Handling	30 TEU/ship hour	15 men/hour	100.000*15/30	50.000 men/hour
Container yard	100.000 TEU	26 men/year	Survey	27 men/year
Storage/distribution	900.000 TEU	540 men /year	540/9	60 men/year
Rail transport (20% traffic)	20% * 900.000 =180.000	54 men year	54/9	6 men year
Road transport (80% traffic)	80% * 900.000 =720.000	480.000 men days	480000/9	227 men year
Port authority	900.000 TEU	680 men year	680/9	75 men year
Container repair and storage	900.000 TEU	400 men year	400/9	44 men year
Shipping agencies	900.000 TEU	1140 men year	1140/9	126 men year
Forwarding and customs	900.000 TEU	1325 men year	1325/9	147 men year
Marine services	2700 Ships	270 men year	270/9	30 men year
Administrative functions	900.000 TEU	365 men year	365/9	41 men year
Total	808 men year			

Table 4.2 – Direct Employment Generated by the Port of Le Havre in 2000

Indirect impact: The impact on industries and institutions that have decided to locate their activities near or around the port, because of their dependence on the port. Examples include factories importing or exporting through the port, logistics and distribution centres processing cargo that passes through the port and traders and financial institutions servicing the various users of the port. The indirect impact declines as the distance from the port increases, a concept called the *gravitation effect*.

Induced impact: The aggregation of the direct and indirect impacts on other sectors of the economy is referred to as the induced impact. The input of one branch of the economy is an output for another branch and is known as the *multiplier effect*. For instance, one additional income or salary in cargo handling results in expenses for consumers and revenues. For the providers in developed countries, induced revenues (impacts) can reach as far as 50% of new revenues (investments and projects).

The measurement of port impacts is performed through macro-economic empirical analyses and may use input-output tables. As shown in Figure 4.1 the methods used for estimating port impacts are not harmonised among world ports. The most common measure used at present is the *aggregate added-value (AV)* of a port project or investment. Examples are shown in Table 4.3. Other popular methods include the *mass calculation* method, used when detailed data is not available or reliable and the *weighted-flows* method, when the estimates of the impact are weighted against various factors and linked to geographical criteria.

Examples of factors used in the weighted flows method include the port's contribution in the creation of new jobs and economic activities, the generation of taxes and additional revenues for local or central governments, the improvement of the balance of trade (trade supply/deficit) and the balance of payments (supply of hard currencies) and the development of cities and regions (spatial economics).

Port	Origins of Information	Method of Calculation	Geographic area	Typology
Nantes/Nazaire (France)	Firms' accounts, Survey	Weighted flows	West Region (Loire)	Port operations, activities and services in the industrial zone
Dunkirk (France)	Firms accounts, Official statistics, port surveys	Mass aggregation	City and suburbs	Industrial activities, fishing, and other services
Belgian ports	National surveys, national accounts (balances of trade and payments)	Mass calculations for industrial activities Weighted flows for service sectors	Port zone	All private and public activities in the defined port zone
Rotterdam (Netherlands)	National accounts	Mass calculations	City and suburbs	Direct, indirect and induced

Figure 4.1 – The use of Methods for Measuring Port Impacts

(Source: ISEMAR, France)

Port	Year	AV/task force	AV/Ton
Dunkirk	1993	120 000 $	60 000 $
Nantes/Nazaire	1995	118 000 $	72 000 $
Antwerp	1995	140 000 $	69 000 $
Gent	1995	105 000 $	142 000 $
Bruges/Zeebruge	1995	84 000 $	31 000 $
Rotterdam	1993	88 000 $	121 000 $

Table 4.3 – Examples of Direct and Indirect Added Value (AV) in European Port Investment

4.6 FUNDING AND FINANCING PORT PROJECTS AND INVESTMENTS

One of the major issues of port management is to identify and seek available sources of funding for ports' projects and investments. The port industry is by essence capitalistic, that is it requires expensive infrastructure, huge investment and capital resources to be able to compete successfully. Financing arrangements not only determine the approach for investment appraisal, but may also create a comparative advantage in favour of, or detrimental to the port. For instance, a port that enjoys good leverage, free or easy preferential access to financial markets will gain a competitive advantage against other ports.

Over a long period of time, port managers have relied mainly on subsidies from the public sector for building port infrastructure, and improving their equipment and facilities. As subsidies were not included in port financial statements, port managers could exhibit very positive financial results. *Government funding* and *retained earnings* have been the most common source of port finance. Government funding can take many forms ranging from grants (either local, national; or through bilateral or multilateral co-operation between countries), to preferential access to capital markets where ports enjoy for instance tax-exempt bonds or low interest rate loan schemes. Retained earnings refer to a widely approved method in infrastructure projects, whereby the profit of port activities is retained to finance future investment projects.

Today, the presence of the private sector in the port industry has increased significantly in both developed and developing countries. Private banks have rarely invested in port infrastructure projects, either solely or through syndication. Private funding for port infrastructure developments has largely been limited to international lending institutions such as the World Bank and other regional banks for example the African Development Bank or Asian Development Bank. Due to the policy of port privatisation the last decade has however seen large scale private investments in port superstructure, handling equipment and storage facilities. The evolving trends are arrangements around complex and multi-dimensional Public and Private Partnership (PPP) arrangements and between public port entities and private investors (Private Equity Schemes). As the private sector involvement in port projects has increased, so have the legal and economic tools that finance and regulate them. The World Bank has enumerated seven elements which are shaping the nature of the private sector involvement in ports:

1. Expected yield.

2. Debt/equity financing structure.

3. Sponsorship.

4. Legality of contracts.

5. Transparency.

6. Fair and open bidding procedures.

7. Feasibility studies (technical, financial, economic and environmental).

Private Investment in Ports

The increasing role of private enterprise in the port sector has given rise to a large variety of funding and management schemes for port projects and investments. The most prominent of these are the various forms of leasing and concession arrangements.

Leasing is a method by which an agreement is made for the right to use an asset for example land or equipment, over an agreed period of time in return for payment. Payment can be a single one-off transaction or made in a series of instalments. In practice there are many variations of leasing agreements, but two forms are dominant:

1. **Lease Contract**, where an operator enters into a long-term lease on port land, superstructure and equipment.

2. **Leasehold Agreement** is a leasing contract, with only port land or warehouse facilities being the subject of the lease. Sometimes berths are included in the lease.

There are various ways in which the lease will be paid. The main methods of lease payment are flat rate, minimum/maximum rate and shared revenue.

- **Flat rate leases** are used when the right to use a fixed asset during a specific period of time is compensated for by periodical payments of a fixed amount of money.

- **The minimum-maximum (mini-max) rate** is practiced when lease payments are variable depending on the level of activity. The varying amounts should lie between minimum and maximum figures that are established in advance.

- **Shared revenue** leases are similar to the mini-max rate, apart from excluding the maximum ceiling amount. In a shared revenue lease, there is a minimum payment regardless of the level of activity, but no maximum payment.

Concession Arrangements are variants of port financing. In a concession the contracting government maintains ownership of the port land but grants the concessionaire the right to finance, build and operate a facility or some equipment, for public use, for a stated period of time. The concessionaire not only covers the costs of investment but assumes all commercial risks. After the agreed time has lapsed the facility or the equipment may or may not be transferred to the concessionaire .The purpose of granting a concession is to increase private financial participation in the development of the port without changing the structure of the port status. Concessions can be seen as a temporary form of privatisation. The arrangements of port concessions and their relationship with port ownership is further developed in Chapter Ten.

4.7   RISK AND RISK MANAGEMENT IN PORT INVESTMENT PROJECTS

Risk is the possibility that an investment will not perform as anticipated. Risk and risk management are inherent in all types of projects and fields of economic activity. However, risk management in ports may have other dimensions given the complexity of the port business and, in particular, the omni-presence of the public authority throughout the various stages of investment, operations, and management. The concept of risk sharing between the private investor (operator) and the public regulator has emerged in recent years and underlines the essence of public-private-partnership management in ports. The involvement of private companies in port management can take place through various, complex and multi-dimensional partnership arrangements with the port public authority. This requires the establishment of a clearly defined contractual framework which enables port investors to quantify and later manage the risks they will be confronted with. The following risk items need to be considered in most port investment projects. There are three dominant areas of risk in Port Investment:

1.   Cost Risk

2.   Revenue Risk

3.   Country Risk

Cost Risk is the risk of exceeding initial cost estimates. In ports, this may stem from the changes imposed by the technical, economic, and financial legal framework, as well as from the changes in social and environmental regulations. The nature and level of the risk also varies depending on the definition of the investment or the project. If this latter is considered as of a public service or priority, it is unlikely that the regulation will change drastically during the project's implementation, and thus the derived risk will be relatively low. If, on the other hand, the investment or service undertaken by the operator is considered of a private nature, then the risk may be significant, and thus the investor will have either to include it in cost calculations (risk integration) and pass it on to ultimate users, or to share it with the public authority through guarantee or compensation arrangements.

Revenue Risk is the commercial risk taking place when revenues are below the estimates. It is the principal risk involved in a port project, due to the uncertainty inherent in traffic and throughput predictions. In principle, the revenue risk is not shared by the public entity since revenues earnings go solely to the private investor. There are however examples when risk sharing can take place, such as in situations of public service monopoly.

Country Risks refer to the risks resulting from the national and international port environment within which a project or an investment is implemented and managed. The most common country risks an operator has to consider prior and during the project's implementation are political risk, social risk, legal risk, monetary risk, economic risk, and force majeure, or the risk stemming from exceptional circumstances such as natural disasters

In conclusion accounting and budgeting control systems (financial statements) are designed to assess the financial performance of port operations and management, whereas financial and economic appraisal tools are used to assess the feasibility and profitability of port investments and development projects. In both cases, ports need to establish their financial control systems in line with their financial targets and long-term strategies. In particular, ports must examine the different funding alternatives, and evaluate the derived risks before authorising a project or endorsing an investment plan. Financial control management must continuously accompany the different phases of a project's implementation, while a post-investment evaluation is highly recommended after the project's completion. A typical evaluation check-list for capital port projects is shown below.

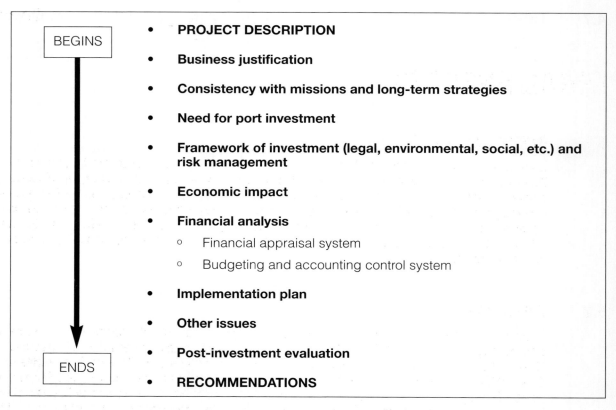

Figure 4.2 – Capital Project Evaluation Checklist

4.8   SELF-ASSESSMENT AND TEST QUESTIONS

Attempt the following and check your answers from the text.

1.   Define and explain the importance of 'depreciation' in financial accounting. Why is an understanding of particular value to a port manager.

2.   Discuss the role of ratio analysis in evaluating the financial strengths and weaknesses of a port organisation.

3.   What is meant by the term 'opportunity cost'?

4.   Explain the discounted cash flow approach to the financial appraisal of ports.

5.   What is the purpose of undertaking an economic appraisal of a port development project?

6.   Describe the role of private finance schemes in port development.

Having completed Chapter Four attempt the following and submit your answers to your Tutor.

1.   The use of financial ratios helps port managers to understand the strengths and weaknesses of their organisation and take appropriate strategic action. Discuss.

2.   Fully explain why it is necessary to undertake an economic analysis in addition to a financial analysis when evaluating the potential of a capital project in a port.

Chapter 5

LEGAL ASPECTS

5.1   INTRODUCTION

Law is a social science which provides a framework for relationships between individuals, businesses and the wider community. It is a complex area to study. Chapter Five will provide some insight into the legal issues which are of concern to port management. Port management is principally concerned with two areas of the law namely; Criminal Law which concerns offences against the state and Civil Law which covers the rights and duties of individuals towards each other. A port is provided with statutory powers to ensure that imposition of regulation is open and accountable.

5.2   GENERAL

A port is located within the jurisdiction of a single state but interfaces with the international community. A port lies within the territorial waters of the coastal state and will have to recognise Conventions decided at international level. The United Nations Convention on the Law of the Sea (UNCLOS) gives the coastal state powers to enforce national standards within its territorial seas. The specialised agency of the United Nations which is responsible for developing international standards concerning safety and pollution prevention is the International Maritime Organization (IMO). The IMO has forty Conventions, and protocols relating to its area of responsibility. In addition the IMO has produced numerous Codes such as the International Safety Management Code (ISM). Nation states who are signatories to a Convention will ratify the Convention into its own statutory system through Acts of Parliament and associated Statutory Instruments. Once ratified a convention can be enforced through an agency of the nation state. The Marine and Coastguard Agency (MCA) of the United Kingdom has enforcement powers, either as the Flag State or Port State.

FLAG, PORT AND COASTAL STATE JURISDICTION

The **FLAG STATE** is responsible for the enforcement of international regulations on board a ship which is registered and flies the flag of that state. As a ship enters zones closer to the coast the influence of the Coastal State increases.

PORT STATE refers to the state of the port in which a ship is berthed. The Port State can inspect a ship and if found to be in breach of rules of an International Convention can take action.

RIGHTS OF THE COASTAL STATE If there is clear evidence of infringement of regulations of the coastal state, the coastal state may institute proceedings against the ship.

The legal identity of port ownership can be categorised in one of several ways. In the United Kingdom there are three dominant models of port ownership. Each model establishes the duties and responsibilities of the port to different stake holders. The foremost model is the company owned (private) port. Trust ports and ports owned by a municipality are also of importance.

Company owned ports lie within the private sector and are subject to the full freedoms and disciplines of the market place. As with any private company they are free to look for commercial funding for investment. Management of company owned ports have to account to shareholders for their performance. Shareholders expect a return on their investment in terms of income (dividends) or growth of share value. The private ownership of ports is gaining ground. **Trust ports** are run by an independent statutory body in which a board of trustees are charged with acting in the interests of all port 'stakeholders'. Surplus of incomes raised are reinvested back into the port infrastructure. The port is not owned by the trust. **Municipal ports** are owned and managed by local authorities for the benefit of the community and will aim to achieve a balance between income and costs and the avoidance of subsidy.

Any port authority has to be knowledgeable about legislation concerning:

- Planning

- Employment

- Health and Safety at Work

- Environmental Protection

- Marine Safety

- Dangerous Substances

- Port Security

Beyond company law, specific Parliamentary Acts establish the legal responsibilities of port authorities. The table below lists the principal Parliamentary Acts which apply to United Kingdom ports and merchant shipping.

KEY UK PRIMARY PORT AND SHIPPING LEGISLATION

Principal Port Acts

Harbours Docks & Piers Clauses Act 1847
Coast Protection Act 1949
Harbours Act 1964
Health and Safety at Work Act 1974
Transport Act 1981
Public Health (Control of Diseases) Act 1984
Dangerous Vessels Act 1985
Food and Environment Protection Act 1985
Ports Act 1991
Transport and Works Act 1992
Marine Safety Act 2003
Town and Country Planning Act

Principal Merchant Shipping Acts

Hovercraft Act 1968
Carriage of Goods by Sea Act 1971-1992
Pilotage Act 1987
Aviation and Maritime Security Act 1990
Merchant Shipping Act 1995
Merchant Shipping and Maritime Security Act 1997

5.3   PLANNING

The need to plan major infrastructure projects is critical as they have an impact on the regional and national infrastructure and economy. Planning for the development of ports is important and is undertaken in accordance with the planning procedures of the nation state. Port development is expensive and long term. Port water frontage is scarce and resources once committed to development cannot be used elsewhere. In the privatised port environment free competition between ports can lead to conflict and waste. A centralised port planning environment can lead to port policy decisions which are slow to respond to market needs. Debate concerning the merits and demerits of centralised port planning and a privatised free market approach to port planning continues.

The United Kingdom has attempted to deal with the conflicts between the two approaches to planning since the end of World War II. Presently the privatised free market approach is used. Complications in port planning are created by the scale of land area required and the supporting road and rail infrastructure needed to support a port development. The United Kingdom is a relatively small island which has more than one hundred and twenty commercially active ports, an overlap between the traditional port hinterlands and a dense road system. Present policy in the UK allows the market to determine where port development should take place. That said any new development will be subject to planning procedures exercised under the Town and Country Planning Act (1990) Planning procedures for port development will require a Planning Inquiry to take place which will cover environmental issues, safety needs, impact studies on the local and regional economy, and the accessibility and integration of the development to the regional plan. Recently the UK Government has reviewed the rules and procedures (covered by the Town and Country Planning Act) for processing major infrastructure projects with the aim of reducing the time given to an Inquiry.

A Planning Inquiry is guided by the principles of openness, fairness and impartiality. It is run by a Lead Inspector who invites the major participants concerned with the development to give and hear evidence for and against the proposal. A Technical Adviser may be appointed to provide an independent report on the proposed project which will be available to the inquiry, but its findings will not be binding. At the conclusion of a Planning Inquiry the Inspector will make his report with his recommendations to the Secretary of State. The final decision lies with the Secretary of State. Appeals against any decision can be made. Planning procedure can be long and expensive. A recent Planning Inquiry into the development of a new container terminal at Dibden Bay, Southampton cost more than £40 Million and took eight years to complete. The proposal was finally rejected on environmental grounds. The proposer did not appeal against the decision partly on grounds of cost. Planning procedures for port development will vary across the world with different nation states having their own planning policies and rules.

5.4   EMPLOYMENT

Whilst changes in technology have lessened the demand for port workers, without port workers a port could not function. A port employer needs to be familiar with employment law. Employment Law is made up of common law and statute law and describes the rights and duties of employer and employee. In accepting work from an employer a contract is made. For a Contract of Employment to be valid the normal principles of contract apply. At its most basic an offer needs to be made and acceptance agreed. An employer does not have to give the employee a written contract, or if they do it may not necessarily cover all the details of their employment. However, an employee is entitled to an Employment Statement, which describes the agreement. Duties placed on the port employer by an agreement with a port worker can be extensive. For example the requirement to provide remuneration in exchange for labour may go beyond pay for services undertaken. Employment Law can establish the need for holiday pay, sick pay, pay during suspension and pay during statutory time off for example; attending to Trade Union matters. Other issues concerning Employment Law cover sex and racial discrimination, equal pay for equal work, termination of a contract of employment and protection against unfair dismissal, The duties required of the port worker are to use all reasonable skill and care at work, to give faithful service (known as the 'duty of fidelity') and to respect confidential information acquired during employment. A port employer is liable for damage caused by an employee to another person during his employment. This is known as **vicarious liability**.

5.4.1   Employment Relations Act

Unions exist to support and represent their members. In former days unions representing the port worker in the United Kingdom were very powerful and could cause national disruption to exports and imports by strike action. Wildcat strikes were particularly damaging. In order to provide a framework in which industrial disputes could be sensibly resolved and actions made lawful the Employment Relations Act has been established. The Employment Relation's Act provides the legal recognition of trade unions, describes the rights of trade union members, workers and employers, enforces the minimum wage and considers issues relating to the administration of union activity. In the ports industry the Employment Relations Act has capped wildcat strikes and has provided a framework by which employer and worker disputes can be resolved.

5.5 HEALTH AND SAFETY AT WORK

Health and Safety legislation has been in existence since the beginning of the nineteenth century. It grew in a piecemeal fashion and by the latter half of the twentieth century was patchy and overcomplicated. In 1972 an Inquiry headed by Lord Robens was set up to report on matters concerning the health, safety and welfare of people at work. The legislative result of the completed report was the Health and Safety at Work Act 1974 (HASAWA 1974) The Act provided a single approach to legislation in the field of industrial safety and health. Where appropriate specialised regulation (eg the Dock Regulations 1988) or Codes of Practice were developed. The broad aims of the Act are to secure the health, safety and welfare of people at work, to protect persons other than persons at work against risks to their health and safety, to control the keeping and use of explosives and dangerous substances and to control the emission into the atmosphere of noxious or offensive substances. The duties of both the employer and employee are described in the Act and are stated below. A port authority is responsible to all users of the port and is required to 'assess the level of risk against the cost of eliminating that risk in deciding whether reasonable steps have been taken'.

The employers specific duties under the HASAWA are to:

- provide and maintain safe plant and work systems.

- ensure the safe use, handling, storage and transportation of articles.

- provide information instruction training and supervision.

- provide a safe working environment without health risks.

- provide adequate welfare facilities.

- ensure that the public are not exposed to risk.

- make no charge for equipment provided for the employees safety.

- provide a written safety policy.

- consult safety representatives and establish a safety committee.

- prevent noxious gases entering the atmosphere.

- maintain appropriate records.

The employees specific duties under the HASAWA are to:

- take reasonable care for themselves and others.

- co-operate with the employer as far as necessary for the execution of the employers duties.

- refrain from intentionally or recklessly interfering with anything provided for health safety or welfare.

Failure to act reasonably to ensure the health safety and welfare of employees at work can result in criminal prosecution, may lead to the employee suing the employer for personal injury, or in extreme cases the employer being prosecuted for corporate manslaughter. Employers must have a written policy on health and safety at work which must be provided to all employers. Failure to provide the policy is an offence punishable in a magistrates court to a fixed fine and if taken to the Crown Court an unlimited fine. The Health and Safety at Work Act has created two statutory bodies, the Health and Safety Commission and the Health and Safety Executive (HSE). The Health and Safety Commission is responsible for promoting research and training into health and safety matters at work, and the provision of information and advice concerning carrying out major investigations. The Health and Safety Executive's main function is the enforcement of statutory law within the workplace.

It was once considered that the law established under the Merchant Shipping Acts concerning health and safety matters onboard UK Merchant ships and all ships in UK ports should be subsumed under HASAWA. However the idea was rejected due to mass and complication of legislation involved. In a UK port health and safety legislation is considered separately under the HASAWA for port workers and under the Merchant Shipping Act for seafarers.

In port areas accidents may occur onboard ship. Under the Merchant Shipping Act 1995, the UK Marine Accident Investigation Branch (MAIB) is responsible for the investigation of marine accidents which occur onboard UK ships world-wide, and on other ships which are in UK territorial waters. The objective of a MAIB investigation is to determine the circumstances and causes of the accident with a view to preserving life and avoiding future accidents. The MAIB does not apportion blame or liability. The powers of MAIB inspectors, and the framework for reporting and investigating accidents, are set out in the Merchant Shipping Act 1995. and are put into effect by the Merchant Shipping (Accident Reporting and Investigation) Regulations. The regulations are the foundation of the MAIB's work and apply to merchant ships, fishing vessels and (with some exceptions) pleasure craft. They define accidents, set out the purpose of investigations, lay down requirements for the reporting of accidents and establish the conduct and investigation of an accident. A Memorandum of Understanding exists between the Health and Safety Executive (HSE), the MAIB and the Maritime Coastguard Agency (MCA) as to which organisation will take the lead in an investigation where common interests are shared.

Directives produced by the European Union (EU) are increasingly being incorporated in UK law with respect to health and safety at work. Significant areas of European regulation involving the ports industry are the management of risk assessment, the work place environment, manual handling of cargoes and personal protection.

5.5.1 Dock Regulations (1988)

The Docks Regulations are specialist regulations based on the International Labour Organisation (ILO) Convention 152, and, in the United Kingdom, established under the Health and Safety at Work Act. They aim to provide safe working conditions in port areas. The regulations cover port operations in which shore based port workers are involved. The regulations are enforced by the Health and Safety Executive. Laid out in the regulations are the duties of the port employer, terminal operators and port employees. The Dock Regulations do not place any duty on the Master or crew of a ship whose responsibilities are described in the Merchant Shipping Act. The employer of a port worker has a duty to ensure that the planning and execution of port operations is undertaken in a manner that does not cause danger to the employee.

Sections contained in the Docks Regulations cover the following areas:

- lighting (adequate lighting helps prevent accidents).

- access and fencing within a dock area.

- transport by water within a dock area.

- the provision of suitable rescue and lifesaving equipment, fire-fighting equipment and means of escape from danger.

- hatches, ramps and car decks. (misuse of equipment can lead to serious injury or death).

- drivers of vehicles and operators of lifting appliances. (Drivers should be trained, fit, competent and over 18 years of age).

- use of vehicles. (The use of vehicles in ports can cause danger. The regulations state that dangers can be reduced by providing adequate roadways and control systems in dock areas).

- use, testing, marking and examination of lifting plant. (Lifting equipment can fail if not properly used and maintained. This can lead to injury or death).

- confined spaces. (Gases can accumulate in confined spaces. Oxygen starvation can also occur. Both can overcome a person entering the space often with tragic consequences).

- welfare amenities. (Under the Docks Regulations the port employer has to provide welfare facilities, including feeding, washing, sanitary and medical facilities for the employee. The employer is required to provide protective clothing, including safety helmet and high visibility garments).

- duty to report defective plant. (All employees have the duty to report defects in the plant being used).

- certificates and reports. (It is a requirement that the employer has to maintain adequate records and certificates of activities associated with the Dock Regulations).

5.6   ENVIRONMENTAL PROTECTION

A port is sensitive to environmental damage. Port Managers have many legal responsibilities to maintain the environment. Associated British Ports (ABP) have established an Environmental Management System concerning ten environmental themes. The themes cover air quality, biodiversity, climate change, dredging, estate management, integrated coastal zone management, resource management, sustainable transport networks and port development, waste management and water quality management. For each theme, the legislation in force is considered and the issues which impact on management are established. Policy guidelines and goals are developed which have to be achieved by the port manager. Environmental legislation is based on international conventions, such as the International Convention for the Prevention of Pollution from Ships (MARPOL 73/78), European Directives, such as the Habitats Directive and a diverse range of Parliamentary Acts and Regulations including the Coast Protection Act (1949) and the Dangerous Vessels Act (1985).

MARPOL 73/78 provides regulations to prevent pollution by ship caused by:

- Oil

- Noxious liquid substances in bulk

- Harmful substances carried by sea in packaged forms

- Sewage from ships

- Garbage from ships

- Air pollution from ships

A port has particular responsibilities to support ships fulfil their environmental responsibilities through the provision of adequate waste management plans and slop facilities for oil residues, oily mixtures and other liquid noxious substances. Ships are not permitted to dispose of plastic wastes at sea. Garbage reception facilities will be required at ports, the scale and type of which will be assessed by the port authority based on the needs of ships which call. Port State control inspectors are able to test that ship's crews are able to carry out procedures relating to marine pollution prevention, inspect onboard records relating to pollutants and examine onboard equipment used to reduce waste and pollution.

In ports, dredging can cause environmental damage in the short or long term. through impact on water quality, natural habitats, bathymetry and physical processes. Disposal of dredged material (spoil) needs consideration by the port authority. If the disposal of spoil is undertaken at sea it will be subject to the rules of the Convention on the Prevention of Pollution by Dumping of Waste and Other Material (1972) known as the London Dumping Convention. The Convention has been adopted by the dredging industry and enables a correct assessment to be made regarding the suitability for dumping dredged material at sea.

One concern of environmental importance is the occasional need for a ship to seek a place of refuge when in difficulties. If the ship is a laden tanker environmental risks to the coastal state are present. If the internal waters in which refuge is sought lie within port limits, port management will be involved. The right of a ship to enter port or internal waters of another state in situations of *force majeure* is not regulated by United National Convention on the Law of the Sea, UNCLOS, but guidelines (Guidelines on Places of Refuge for Ships in Need of Assistance) have recently been established by the IMO.

Port authorities have a legal duty to respond to oil spill on their waters, but unless the port harbour authority owns the land, shoreline clear-up is the responsibility of the local authority.

The International Safety Management Code (ISM Code) recognises that ships should liaise with port authorities to prevent pollution through the use of ship shore check-lists, harbour watches and patrols and if an incident occurs, such as an accidental spillage, agreed procedures are used to minimise the impact.

5.7   MARINE SAFETY

The Port Marine Safety Code (PMSC) was developed in 2000 to improve the safety of those who work in ports, It also concerns, ships, passengers and the environment. The PMSC establishes a system by which harbour authorities are accountable to the public for delivering a UK national standard for safe marine operations in ports. The Port Marine Safety Code was drawn up following a review of the 1987 Pilotage Act to promote best practice. It describes the position of the harbour authority for port safety. It covers their duties with respect to the appointment of the Harbour Master. It makes transparent the responsibilities of the Chief Executive, Harbour Master and port officers for marine safety. The Code covers aspects of risk assessment and safety management including the need for a safety management system, and an emergency planning and risk assessment. Conservancy responsibilities include comment on the provision of navigation aids and Vessel Traffic Services (VTS). Pilotage is covered in some detail. The provision of marine services in ports, such as tugs, pilot launches, workboats and moorings are also covered in the Code. Overall the PMSC covers the Harbour Authorities legal duties and powers to ensure safety in their waters.

5.8   DANGEROUS SUBSTANCES

The UK Dangerous Goods in Harbour Areas Regulations (1987) is a Statutory Instrument which describes the legal responsibility of the harbour authority and terminal operators regarding the handling of dangerous substances. The regulations require that notice is given prior to dangerous goods entering a harbour area. The powers of the Harbour Master to prohibit the entry or movement of dangerous substances in the harbour area are described. Other areas covered include the:

- marking and navigation of vessels carrying dangerous substances.

- responsibilities of employers to employees handing dangerous substances.

- safe handling of liquid dangerous substances in bulk including chemical and liquefied gas.

- packaging and labelling of freight containers containing packaged dangerous substances.

- Emergency arrangements including the need for the preparation of emergency plans by the harbour authority and emergency arrangements on the berth.

- The storage of dangerous substances in port areas including storage tanks, storage of freight containers and the parking of road vehicles carrying dangerous substances.

The final substantive area of regulation covers the handling of explosive cargoes. The regulations are strict and describe the need for licensing, security arrangements and the control of the movement of dangerous goods within a port area.

5.9 PORT SECURITY

Ports and ships are vulnerable to abuse by third parties. Illegal immigrants and asylum seekers seeking entry to a considerate nation will in most circumstances enter through a port. A greater potential threat to a port is that of terrorist activity, a threat which has been heightened by the attack on the World Trade Centre on September 11th 2001 (9/11).

Ports have had to take the threat of terrorist attack seriously. Certain countries had port security legislation in place prior to 9/11. For example the UK Aviation and Maritime Security Act was established in 1990. The IMO had approved guidelines to prevent unlawful acts against passengers and crews following the hijacking of ships.

The 9/11 attack confirmed weaknesses in the international shipping and ports industries regarding security. Following 9/11 the International Ship and Port Facility Security Code (ISPS Code) was established. The Code is embodied in Chapter Eleven of the Safety of Life at Sea Convention. (SOLAS 1974)

After 9/11 the vulnerability of an attack on nation states through ships and ports was realised. There are three major areas of concern:

1. A terrorist attack upon a ship.

2. The use of the ship as a delivery system for a terrorist attack within a port.

3. The use of cargo (containers) used as a delivery system for targets away from the port.

The ISPS Code has six sections covering the joint responsibilities of the port and shipping industry to help reduce risk. The sections concern:

- Ship modifications and Additional Carriage Requirements.

- Shipping Company Responsibilities.

- Documentary Requirements for Ships.

- The ISPS Code in Operation – Compliance and Controls.

- Obligations of Contracting Governments.

- Requirements for Ports.

5.9.1 The Ship and Security

Ships are required to carry an Automatic Identification System (AIS), have a Ship Security Alert System (SSAP), appoint a security officer, have carried out a security assessment and produce a security plan. In addition ships are required to have 'on-board' security information relating to ports of call and maintain a continuous 'synopsis record' of security issues and ports visited. Documentary information relating to crew, the charter party and those responsible for deciding the ships employment has to be carried and will be required on entry to a port. The level of security alert established by the port state is to be made known to ships entering or intending to enter a port. Ships such as cruise ships may be instructed not to enter ports which have declared a high level of security alert. The port has the right to control the movement of ships in and those intending to enter port. Specific to ports are requirements concerning the use of firearms in combating terrorism in port areas.

5.9.2 The Port and Security

As far as ports are concerned, the ISPS code is applicable to port facilities serving ships greater than 500 gt engaged on international voyages. Contracting governments are given the option to extend the application of the Code to other types of ports and terminals. The Code sets three security levels ranging from low to high in proportion to the nature and scope of the incident or the perceived security threat. Ports and port authorities are required to develop and implement a Port Facility Security Plan (PFSP) for each level of alert. The port will designate a Port Facility Security Officer (PFSO) and provide appropriate training, drills and exercises for the PFSO and other security personnel. The PFSP is related to the outcome of the Port Facility Security Assessment (PFSA). Unlike ships and shipping companies, ports do not require international certification but are required to have a statement of compliance.

Significant non-ISPS security initiatives have been introduced by the United States government and incorporated in the US Maritime Transportation Act (MTS) of 2002. The MTS Act includes port-related measures that go beyond what has been agreed at IMO, including the requirement for security cards for port personnel and the development of a system of foreign port security assessments. The latter requirement empowers the United States authorities to bar access to vessels arriving at its ports from unsafe or blacklisted ports. All foreign ports involved in trading with the United States of America have to comply with the provisions of the ISPS Code

In addition to the demands of the MTS Act, the United States of America has introduced a number of non-binding voluntary programmes for the international shipping community involved in US trade. The measures primarily target vessels and cargoes, but also apply to non-American ports at which a ship (or her cargo) calls prior to reaching US waters. External non-US ports providing inbound cargo for the United States have to comply with these rules or lose the American market. The two main US programmes relevant to ports are the:

- Container Security Initiative (CSI)

- Customs-Trade Partnership Against Terrorism (C-TPAT).

The two schemes introduce a number of rules that aim at improving security against terrorism by targeting the movement of container-cargo (CSI) across the entire supply chain (C-TPAT). Under a C-TPAT partnership agreement, participants need to provide reliable and verifiable security information in exchange for preferential treatment during customs inspections.

Specific C-TPAT initiatives relevant to ports include Operation Safe Commerce (OSC) and the Smart and Secure Tradelanes (SST). The 24-hour 'advance vessel manifest rule' or the '**24-hour rule**' is a major security requirement under which carriers or their agents have to submit a cargo declaration for each US bound container 24 hours before loading at the foreign port. This measure, is applicable to containers both transited by and imported into the US. It is probably the most controversial of all initiatives as conflicts with the optimisation of the logistics chain and can impact on operational flexibility. The '24 hour rule' has the potential to distort competition between different market players, including ports.

The narrative above covers some of the important legal aspects associated with port operational management. Economic regulation of ports is determined at a political level. At a strategic level within the port contractual relationships and statutory responsibilities will follow the national process. At a local level harbour authorities have powers devolved from Parliament in the form of private bills and harbour orders to impose statutory requirements in relation to marine safety, marine pollution prevention and efficient use of the port.

5.9.3 The UK Ports Policy Review

In 2004 the UK Government undertook to review the policy framework for ports which resulted in the UK Ports Policy Review being launched in 2006. The Review recognises that the UK Government is involved with port development due to their impact on the economy, society and environment at local, regional and national levels. The key issues examined by the Ports Policy Review cover the likely demand for port capacity, how port growth can be developed in a sustainable way, how far Government should reflect regional development objectives in the provision of port capacity and how can Government help smaller ports realise their full potential.

The legal issues raised in the Review concern the regulation of competition in the ports sector, ownership of ports, port safety legislation and improvements of the planning system for ports. The UK Ports Policy Review is on going (2006)

5.10 SELF-ASSESSMENT AND TEST QUESTIONS

Attempt the following and check your answers from the text.

1. Planning a substantive port development can be expensive in time and cost. Describe a planning process with which you are familiar.

2. What is meant by Port State Control?

3. The Dock Regulations have been created to ensure the safety of employees at work. Discuss.

4. Expand the meaning of the abbreviations (i) MARPOL (ii) AIS (iii) PMSC.

5. State the main areas of environmental law which are of concern to a port authority.

6. List the main elements of port security legislation.

Having completed Chapter Five attempt the following and submit your answer to your Tutor.

1. The Law relating to Port Management is complex. Fully discuss the areas of law which have a particular significance to the daily operations of the port.

OR

2. For a port with which you are familiar consider how the law regarding SAFETY and ENVIRONMENTAL PROTECTION has been implemented. List any weaknesses and suggest ways in which improvement can be made.

PORT COMPETITION

6.1   INTRODUCTION

Chapter Six considers the issue of port competition. Traditionally the hinterland of a port was defined by geography and the development of industries. Competition was limited. Recent developments mainly due to the growth of containerisation has led to the need for large capital investment in the port and its supporting infrastructure. This Chapter covers the economic concept of competition, features and elements of port competition and the regulatory framework of port competition.

6.2   ECONOMIC CONCEPTS OF COMPETITION

The economic theory of competition is based on the general assumption that all companies in the market seek to maximize their profits. The interaction between price, product or service and suppliers or producers creates various market patterns, under which competition can take different forms. The types of competition are illustrated in Table 6.1

	Type of Competition	Suppliers and degree of product differentiation	Influence of firms over prices	Marketing methods
	Perfect Competition	Many suppliers identical products/services	None	Commodity exchanges or auctions
Imperfect Competition	**Monopolistic Competition**	Many suppliers Product differentiation	Little	Advertising, quality. Often intense price rivalry
	Oligopoly	Few suppliers Product differentiation	Considerable	Advertising, quality. Rivalry administered prices
	Duopoly	Two suppliers Product differentiation	Considerable	Advertising & public relations
	Monopoly	Single producer No close substitutes	Considerable	Promotional & public relations advertising

(Adapted from John Beardshaw 1984)

Table 6.1 – Different Market Forms

Perfect competition is a theoretical possibility but only occurs when no producer or service provider can affect the market price.

Industries operating under perfect competition have four main characteristics:

1. Large number of buyers and suppliers preventing a single actor from affecting the market,

2. Homogeneous or standardised products that can differentiate the industry,

3. Customers and suppliers well informed about product and quality offered or required,

4. Freedom for customers and suppliers to enter to or exit the market.

In reality most markets are imperfect. Imperfect competition includes duopoly and oligopoly. Monopoly is a situation where no competition is present.

The main sources of imperfect competition arise when cost conditions interfere and where barriers to competition are established. Such sources arise in many situations for example:

- where there are a small number of suppliers,

- in situations where significant economies of large-scale production are present,

- when products or services have patent protection,

- where regulatory barriers precludes competition.

These cases can be clearly identified in the maritime industry at both national and international levels. Thus oligopoly seems to apply in the liner shipping market, with increasing forms of maritime cooperation including mergers, consortia, alliances, and conference systems. A near form of perfect competition appears to govern the tramp shipping markets.

In the port sector the emergence of international container port operators, such as Hutchinson Port Holdings and Dubai Ports, suggest that there is a trend towards monopoly particularly in the area of container cargo handling services.

6.2.1   Structural Analysis of Industries

The status and intensity of competition within a given industry is the result of five basic competitive forces. The competitive forces are:

1.   threat of entry,

2.   threat of substitution,

3.   bargaining power of buyers,

4.   bargaining power of suppliers,

5.   rivalry among current competitors.

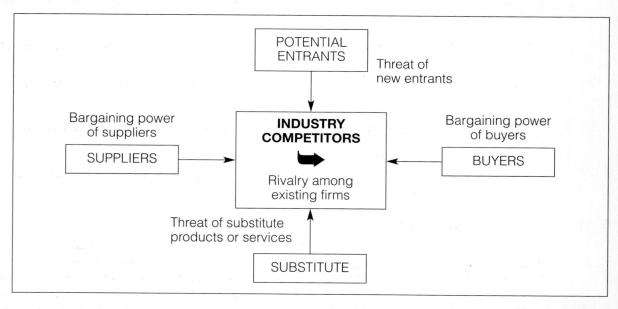

(M. Porter 1980)

Figure 6.1 – Forces Driving Industrial Competition

A general model which drives industrial competition is shown in Figure 6.1. and is valid for different segments of the port industry such as container ports, bulk ports and ferry ports, An understanding by port management of the competitive forces which exists in a particular situation is essential for strategy formulation.

6.3 FEATURES AND ELEMENTS OF PORT COMPETITION

Until the late 1970s most ports in the world were run and managed within a relatively limited competitive environment. Geographical location of the port and the depth of its navigational channels were enough to provide the port with a competitive advantage. The combination of the transport system and the organisational structure of ports favoured a situation where ports enjoyed a certain degree of monopoly within a defined and limited hinterland.

The near monopoly position was reinforced by the structure of liner shipping services. Liner shipping was organised in conferences that charged similar freight rates to the different destinations located in the same spatial range, e.g. North Europe or East Mediterranean. Tramp shipping had little impact. At the same time ports were controlled and managed by corporate public institutions that not only provided substantial financial resources and subsidies, but also secured regulatory protection against non-local and foreign port competition.

Over the last three decades, competition among world ports has increased in both scope and nature. Increased competition has occurred due to several factors including:

- globalisation of world trade,

- privatisation of ports,

- unitisation of cargo,

- developments in transport technology,

- application of cargo-handling technology.

As competition between ship operators, intermodal transport organisations and global logistics providers has increased, so has rivalry between ports. Today, competitive advantage is established by the provision of high quality and value added services to ship and cargo interests using the port.

In order to study the different aspects of port competition, an understanding of the following areas is necessary:

- the structure and dynamics of the port business in relation to trade, transport and logistics system,

- the interaction between port management in its different organisational forms, and the port users,

- the regulatory framework that governs the port industry at both national and international levels.

6.3.1 Various Forms of Port Competition

The identification of port competitors and the development of competitive strategies require an initial detailed study of the port's competitive environment. Relevant, updated and reliable information should continuously be gathered and analysed. It needs to cover domestic and international port competitors. In addition any analysis must consider other potential competitors involved in intermodal transport and logistics. Ports face competition from within and outside the port sector.

If port organisation is considered as a unified and aggregate economic activity, competition will occur at two levels:

Horizontal or Inter-Port Competition:

Inter-port competition takes place in the form of a ***direct competition*** with ports situated within a given spatial range, as well as ***indirect competition*** which normally involves organisations from outside the port sector, such as: inland transport modes, freight forwarders and multi-modal transport operators. The development of new trade and logistics patterns involving sea, land and air transport with network and transhipment ports can create competition from ports located outside the immediate spatial range. Inter-port competition does not need to concern all port activities. A port can compete with others for a specific niche of the market (e.g. type of cargo or commodity). Competition does not necessarily have to include all maritime traffic in the region.

Vertical and Cross Competition: (Intermodal Port Competition).

This is initiated by the competition between different modes of transport and does not originate necessarily from ports. A port may lose its market share when its waterway or maritime traffic is being replaced by air or road transport, e.g. land-bridges. Conversely, it will gain more traffic if it invests in inland facilities (both infrastructure and superstructure) that should be efficiently linked to the intermodal transport system.

If port organisation is considered as a platform, bringing together several activities and actors, then the competition will be centred within the port itself. Two forms of competition can be identified at this level:

Segmented Form (or Intra-Port Competition)

Intra-port competition concerns competition between different components of a port organisation. This can either be horizontal, involving port operation within the same core of activity (e.g. stevedoring companies competing with each other), or vertical, involving different types of port operation and operators (e.g. a stevedoring company competing with a logistics provider).

Aggregate Form of Competition

Is a competitive structure which drives every component of the port community into indirect (inter or cross) port competition. The competitiveness of the port as a whole depends on the efficiency of all operation within the port community. If a port operation does not perform well, the efficiency of the whole port will be at stake. It follows that every member of the port community should work in a collaborative spirit, and be aware of the competition originating from outside the port and through other transport modes.

6.3.2   Decisive Factors of Port Competitiveness

Port competition strategy must be built by identifying the sources of competitive advantage. A good technique to understand competitive advantage is to undertake a SWOT analysis. A SWOT analysis considers strengths, weaknesses, opportunities and threats associated with a business. In the case of a port, strengths and weaknesses relate to an internal analysis of the port, while opportunities and threats relate to the analysis of the external environment.

6.3.3   Strengths and Weaknesses

The purpose of the analysis is to determine the strengths and weaknesses of a port *vis-a-vis* existing and potential competitors. When established the known strengths can be maximised and fully exploited. Weaknesses identified in the analysis can be minimised or alleviated. The main factors determining a port's strengths and weaknesses are listed below:

Location

Location concerns the geographical location of the port and its proximity to shippers and consignees, the suppliers and customers of maritime transport. Location interests concern nearness to main sailing routes, location of major industrial zones and areas of high population density.

Nautical Constraints

Ports have nautical constraints which impact on service delivery. Ship's draught is a critical constraint and will limit accessibility of the ship to a port. Some ports are closed ports and can only be accessed through a lock system. Locks impose limitations on length, breadth and draught of the ship. Other nautical constraints include availability of pilot services and tugs, tidal range, location of the berth and weather conditions.

Hinterland Transport Connections

Road and rail transport links, and sometimes pipeline and waterway connections are of critical importance to success of a port. Traditionally hinterland connections were considered as natural or 'granted' factors. Today the port is often involved in decisions associated with road, rail and inland waterway investments which connect the port to its hinterland.

Physical Assets of the Port

Physical assets in terms of facilities and equipment offered by the port will be considered within the analysis. Physical assets include facilities for ships, such as berth availability, provision of shore-based handling equipment and facilities for cargo including warehousing and storage facilities.

Port and Distribution Costs

Port Costs refers to the price of port services and is the result of the combination of ship and cargo costs. Distribution costs are related to the transport cost from the port of discharge to the final destination. Equally costs associated with transport of an export cargo from factory to departure port is a consideration. Shippers and cargo owners usually seek to use ports that charge minimum distribution costs.

Experience and Know-how

The ability of the port to handle different types and forms of cargo, ships and inland vehicles varies. Port experience and stevedoring know-how is an important factor leading to cost efficiency for the port user.

Manpower

Manpower issues involve labour skills and the social environment. A troublesome social climate, lack of professionalism and poor management are examples that can lead to disastrous effects on port reliability and performance.

Performance

The performance of a port is established through the use of productivity and performance indicators.

Adaptability and Resource

A positive, adaptable and resourceful attitude of port management towards meeting the specific and diversified needs of customers is a strength which cannot be underestimated.

Complementary and Value-Added Services

Complementary and value added services may be offered by a port without necessarily being part of its core business. Services may include ship repair and maintenance facilities, specialised cargo storage, extra-logistics activities, extended information technology systems and financial services. Value added services are measured by their contribution to the port, expressed in terms of value per unit of cargo handled (tonnes or TEU). The higher the added-value, the more attractive the port is to the shipper and cargo owner.

6.3.4 Opportunities and Threats

The analysis focuses on the market. It identifies areas of opportunity where the port has competitive advantage which may not have been fully exploited. It also considers areas of threat by which a port can be undermined by its competitors. The factors that are usually taken into consideration when evaluating a port's external environment are:

Market Identification

Markets concern defined service requirements. For liner services the analysis will need to consider the ship type, market changes and shipping services offered by a port. For tramp services, the cargo type and cargo services are analysed.

Assessment of the Port's Customers' Value Chain:

The concept of the value chain is based on the assumption that activities performed by a firm provide value to the customer. The application of the concept in port business relates to the "value added" by the port to its users, mainly the shippers and shipping lines.

> For **shippers** port "value added" services will include cargo storage, cargo consolidation and break of bulk. They will also include labelling, bagging and packaging facilities and information processing.

> For **shipping lines** port "value added" services cover many areas including ship repair and maintenance facilities, bunkering opportunities, victualling provision and agency support.

Technological Assessment:

Technological assessment relates to the follow-up and monitoring of changes in ship technology, vehicle technology, mechanical handling systems, information technology and procedural systems.

Legal and Regulatory Assessment:

An analysis of the legal and regulatory requirements concentrates on issues concerned with safety, security, and environmental matters.

6.3.5 Generic Competitive Strategies

Once a firm or an organisation has analysed the structure of the industry of which it forms a part, and the number and type of existing and potential competitors, it will need to choose one, or a combination of the following competitive strategies:

- Overall Cost Leadership.

- Differentiation.

- Focus.

6.3.6 Overall Cost Leadership

A strategy of overall cost leadership requires aggressive construction of efficient scale facilities, vigorous pursuit of cost reduction, tight cost and overhead control, and cost minimisation in non-core areas, such as research and development, sales force and advertising.

Management control over costs and low comparative costs are the key factors to achieving overall cost leadership. The main advantage of the strategy is that reduced costs protect companies against the bargaining power of customers and the threat of substitution.

An overall cost leadership strategy has drawbacks including the lack of capacity to invest in new equipment, marketing and research. Many world ports enjoy natural cost leadership through low workforce costs, tax breaks, and proximity to customers and suppliers. Cost leadership is not the only consideration in a competitive market. Quality of service, operational safety and overall security are among other factors which will be considered in port choice and are increasingly considered as a source of competitive advantage.

6.3.7 Differentiation

The basis of a strategy of differentiation is to create a unique selling point or number of points, which will establish a clear distinction from other competitors' products or services.

Differentiation can be achieved through customer service, the use of technology, and quality of operation. The strategy of differentiation does not ignore costs, but costs are regarded as a lesser factor. A strategy of differentiation allows market positioning through customer loyalty and lower sensitivity to price. It can be a risky strategy when customers sacrifice loyalty for low cost or where other competitors adapt the same strategy.

Examples of differentiation strategies in ports include services to special cargo and vessels, dedicated terminals, depth of access channels, recognised security standards and quality assurance programmes. Free ports, export processing zones and value-added logistics activities are also used to differentiate ports.

6.3.8 Focus

Focus is a relatively new strategy used by the port sector. Focus is achieved when a port creates a niche or serves a specific customer or port user. Through specialisation, the level of improvement and know-how of a particular form of traffic or operation increases, leading to greater efficiency and reduction in costs. A strategy of focus will attract customers who will become "captive" to the port. If loyalty is not assured a strategy of focus may yield opposite results and occurs when competitors successfully specialise in the same market niche.

6.4 REGULATORY FRAMEWORK OF PORT COMPETITION

Regulations governing the status of ports and their activities differ. Policies and regulations impact on the competitive position and strategies of ports.

European Union (EU) Competition Policy related to port sector is integrated with the desire to develop a free and sustainable approach to transport development.

The EU Port Infrastructure Green Paper(1997) recognised that competition between and within ports of the EU is increasing. The four principles of EU competition policy which shape port law are:

1. free access,

2. fair competition.

3. liberalisation of and access to services,

4. prohibition of subsidies.

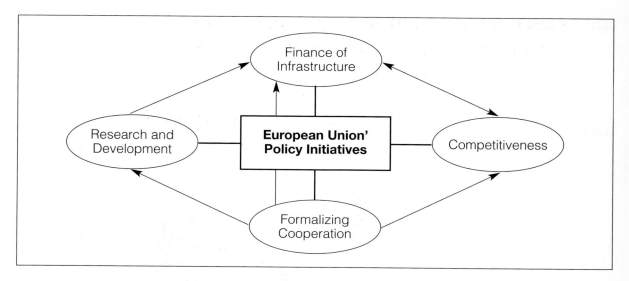

Figure 6.2 – Axes of the EU Port Policy

EU competition policy has had impact on port competition on the four axis shown in Figure 6.2. The axes Include the improvement and modernisation of port infrastructure and its involvement in the Trans-European transport network (Finance of Infrastructure), the creation of a competitive playing field (Competitiveness) the promotion of research and development (Research and Development) and support of dialogue between port, transport and trade partners.(Formalizing Cooperation).

It has been suggested that to date the most successful axis has been that of Research and Development. Major projects have included the optimisation of procedures for berthing and unberthing, loading discharging at seaport terminals, the development of port handling equipment and the provision of information technology. Formalising co-operation has established greater understanding between port authorities, users and service providers. The European Sea Ports Organisation (ESPO) is one organisation which provides a forum where problems relating to port activities can be formally aired.

Environmental Policy will potentially impact on EU port competitiveness. The recent Green Paper EU Maritime Policy (2006) confirms the dependence of the EU on its seaports and recognises the need to promote short sea shipping and Motorways of the Sea within an integrated EU transport system. It also considers the development of maritime transport and environmental conservation. A particular issue needing to be resolved will be the *"question of whether port activities should take place in few very efficient ports connected to the Transport European Networks (TEN-T) or be distributed among a larger number of ports avoiding excessive concentration of activity, with its attendant problems of congestion and pressure on the environment and hinterland infrastructure ?"*

A regulatory framework to enhance port competitiveness and ensure consideration of the port environment is being developed in Europe. In 2001 the European Commission unveiled a paper on improving the quality of port services by increasing open competition in areas such as handling of cargo, piloting and passenger services where the functions were managed by monopoly handlers. Known as the ports' services Directive it was withdrawn in 2006 after having been voted down on two occasions in the European Parliament.

6.5   SELF-ASSESSMENT AND TEST QUESTIONS

Attempt the following and check your answers from the text.

1.   Consider the Port of Lisbon advertisement below.

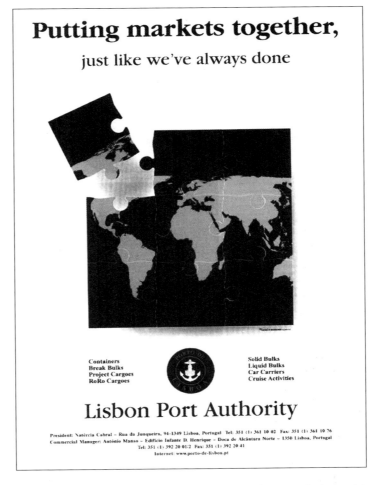

State what you consider the advertisement says about the explicit and implicit strengths of the port.

Suggest reasons for the style of the advertisement used.

2.   Discuss the different competitive strategies which can be adopted by port management.

3.   Compare two ports in close physical proximity to each other (e.g. Rotterdam and Antwerp) and suggest ways in which they strategically seek to distinguish themselves.

4.   How can a free competitive ports environment be reconciled with a national or regionally based ports policy?

Having completed Chapter Six attempt **ONE** of the following and submit your essay to your Tutor.

1.   Critically discuss the main forms of port competition using appropriate examples.

OR

2.   You have been asked to debate the motion:

"the ports industry gains from a free market approach to competition".

Establish an argument with supporting evidence FOR and AGAINST the motion.

Chapter 7

PORT MARKETING

7.1 INTRODUCTION

With the increasing pace of competition among ports, the role of marketing a port has had to develop. Today marketing is an essential part of port management. With all but the smallest of the world's ports having their own marketing departments. Chapter Seven is a simple introduction to Port Marketing and is based on general marketing principles. Marketing of any service involves a number of activities. This Chapter covers the need for information, market research, an understanding of the marketing tools available and consideration of a port promotion strategy.

7.1.1 Port Information

To design a marketing strategy and achieve marketing objectives, port managers need to seek out, gather and analyse relevant and reliable information. As the port environment is complex and constantly changing, market-oriented information has to be extensive and regularly updated.

Marketing information required by a port will need to include data on:

- existing and potential port users

- political, economic, social, and technological developments

- changes in trade patterns and logistic techniques

- current and future developments in other ports

- Regulatory framework and its implications

Marketing Information can be established from a range of sources, including quality commercial newspapers, journals, company accounts and reports. Empirical information can be found in statistics maintained by customs authorities. who in most countries have the responsibility for collecting primary data on import and export traffic. Statistics provided by government departments and international agencies may also be useful. General market intelligence reports written by consultants provide expert comment. Specialised reports may be commissioned by a port to meet particular needs. Other information sources which are available include reports written by the media, professional associations and academic institutions. The use of the world-wide web for gathering and receiving information has revolutionised the intelligence gathering process.

7.1.2 Data Required on Existing and Potential Port Users

It is useful for a port to maintain Information on its 'direct users', such as freight forwarders, agents, and multi-modal transport operators; and 'head users' which include shippers and ship owners.

Business information gathered on port users can cover many areas, including potential developments, new products and services, changes in organisation and management style, business plans and strategic objectives. Information on its own customers will help port management define the user's specific needs and possible future demands on the port.

7.1.3 Information Required about Political, Economic, Social, and Technological Developments Taking Place Including Changes in Trade Patterns and Logistics Techniques

The collection of this form of data is ongoing and will in part be built-up through experience. A methodological approach to data collection of this type is valuable and can be used to inform of likely future changes usually in the medium or longer term.

Political developments increasingly have influence on port activities and strategy 'A recent Review of Ports Policy' in the United Kingdom promoted by the Department for Transport is attempting to establish priorities in an industry where each competitor relies on external infrastructural developments provided by third parties.

Economic data will help inform future market trends and provide port management information regarding variations in import and export cargo volume.

The handling, storage and need for effective inland transport arrangements requires the latest technology to meet the demands of the ports users and external organisations. The role of information technology, the Electronic Data Information systems are now an integral part of port management. Port management need to be alert for new trends in ship type and form as well as in the development of cargo handling equipment and storage needs.

A port is integrated with the social fabric of a community. Changes in port needs will impact on the local population and can cause social disquiet. For example the development of new container terminals many miles from the original port will have a direct impact on labour availability.

Trading patterns change, with new areas of supply and demand having influence on port development. Change can occur rapidly or over the longer term.

7.1.4 Information about the Current and Future Developments in other Ports, Especially Neighbouring Ones

Information about current and future developments in other ports should cover all the aspects affecting the port's competitiveness and market share. Current developments such as the competing ports' cargo performance, financial results, marketing policies, pricing strategies and equipment procurement need to be recognised as they may have a direct implication on the present port strategy.

7.1.5 Information about the Regulatory Framework and its Implications

Whilst ports competition may take place within national boundaries subject to the same regulatory framework, this is not always the case. Many ports compete within a region, as for example ports in the Le Havre – Hamburg range. A knowledge about the regulatory policies associated with each nation and if appropriate each region will need to be understood.

The regulatory framework associated with commercial and industrial developments including government subsidies, support for infrastructure projects and the impact of environmental policy can be competitively significant. Likewise the regulations required to be enforced by statutory bodies such as customs immigration and health authorities may also differ between ports allowing competitive advantage.

7.1.6 Market Research

Market Research is a task that goes beyond information gathering and data collection. It involves the analysis of the information gathered, and the projection of likely future trends.

A useful way to undertake market research is to consider segments of the market (market segmentation). Segmentation of the port market can be looked at in many ways but the following are frequently considered:

- **type of facility**

  including berths and terminals, warehousing and logistics facilities and cargo handling equipment type.

- **traffic and commodity**

  including quantitative analysis of bulk, break-bulk, container, and general-cargo moving through the port.

- **customers and users**

  including information about shipowners, shippers, freight forwarders, and multi-modal transport providers.

The individual form of segmentation undertaken by market research will be determined by the port's marketing and competitive strategies. Segmentation may even be variable within specific categories within a port. For example in the bulk trades it will be desirable to have contact with shippers and cargo interests. It might be advisable for the port to segment its market by number, type, and importance of shippers. The liner trades are dominated by the ocean carriers and hence a focus on the shipping lines, rather than the shippers would be appropriate.

7.1.7   Port Marketing Tools

Marketing tools are elements that influence the 'sale' of a service or product. In the port business, marketing tools can be identified as the 3P's namely: Product, Promotion, and Price. In marketing literature there is normally a fourth P – Place, It is suggested that Place does not apply to ports as they are 'immoveable assets', but location can change in terms of its usefulness and value.

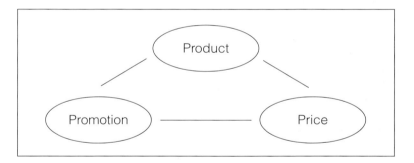

Figure 7.1 – Port Marketing Tools

7.1.8   Product

In port marketing product refers to the range of port operations, services and facilities offered. Apart from price, a user chooses a port based on one or a combination of the following elements: geographical position, navigation approach, hinterland connections, disposition of quays and land area available, the range and quality of port services, efficiency of port labour force, the social climate, management skills and technical know-how, and the fiscal environment. The importance of each element depends on the nature and type of the port's customer or user. Selling points need to be carefully selected to respond to' the needs and expectations of the customer. For example; if the port marketing strategy is to attract a shipping line, then emphasis should be placed on nautical and navigation services, port performance, and ship shore interchange equipment. Emphasis on hinterland connections or intermodal facilities will not need to be so important.

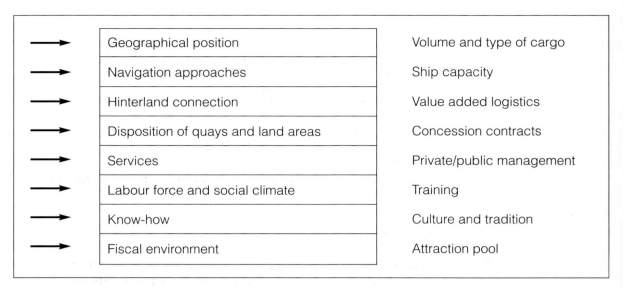

→	Geographical position	Volume and type of cargo
→	Navigation approaches	Ship capacity
→	Hinterland connection	Value added logistics
→	Disposition of quays and land areas	Concession contracts
→	Services	Private/public management
→	Labour force and social climate	Training
→	Know-how	Culture and tradition
→	Fiscal environment	Attraction pool

Figure 7.2 – Marketing Port Services – Influences on the Port Product

7.1.9   Price

A full analysis of pricing techniques and strategies used by ports has been provided in Chapter Five. For the purpose of Chapter Seven discussion is limited to the interaction between price and the marketing of port services. Pricing in ports is very difficult given the wide range of port services, and the complexities generated by the fluctuations in international trade and transport markets. Ports need to undertake certain decisions before marketing or advertising the price of their services. Decisions will be based on estimated costs, competition, currency, payment terms and market demand variables. Information regarding those factors which determine the elements need to be gathered and analysed to help provide a clear pricing strategy.

The pricing of port services is established at different levels and can be segmented for different customers. For the shipowner price segmentation may concern ship type, ship size and number of repeat calls to the port in a period of time.

The most common prices considered by port management include harbour and berthing dues, mooring charges, pilot costs, land leases, handling costs, warehousing, value added services, and auxiliary services such as bunkers and water for ships.

In order to avoid inadequacies and fragmentation, pricing must be simple and coherent. The production of a single document with a comprehensive listing of port tariffs for ship operators and owners is normally available. As price is one element of the marketing mix it is critical that it is competitive with ports in the near proximity.

Shipowners are price sensitive. They are mobile in the sense that commitments to an individual port will endure for a contractual period, but they have freedom to move thereafter. Changes in the port tariff can impact on their decisions regarding the use of a particular port.

Port prices which are set, need to respond to external changes. At the same time they should reflect the strategic decisions of the port concerning estimated costs, competitors costs, currency value, common payment terms associated with international trade and market variables including seasonality and trade cycles. Influences on setting port prices are shown in Figure 7.3. Port prices can be made more attractive to long term customers through the use of discounts and volume rebates.

Estimated Costs
Competition
Currency
Payment terms (INCOTERMS)
Market variables

Figure 7.3 – Marketing Port's Services – Influences on Setting Port Tariff

7.1.10 Promotion

Promotion in port marketing is defined as

"a means of communication between the port and various target groups in order to inform them and influence their market attitudes".

In basic marketing terms promotion concerns advertising, personal selling, sales promotion and publicity. Among the marketing tools available to a firm promotion is probably the most important. Promotion of a port needs to be culture-oriented whilst maintaining the traditional dimension of its own roots.

Promotion is important because whilst a firm may perform the marketing-support functions well (such as research, service provision and effective pricing strategies), without informing the customer base of these functions it is unlikely it will achieve its full potential.

Promotion is the most visible activity of the port marketing process. Its success or failure will depend directly on the assessment and judgement of the customer.

7.1.11 Port Promotion Strategy

A port promotion strategy will consider THREE principal components:

1. means of communication,

2. nature of the audience to be addressed,

3. characteristics of the services to be promoted.

The mix of components used to meet a specific need will require judgement. The means of communications are varied and are sometimes referred to as "promotion tools".

7.1.12 Port Promotion Tools

The choice of promotion tools available to port management are many and varied. The use of a specific promotion tool or mix of promotion tools will vary and depend on the specific task to be undertaken. In addition it will be influenced by the scale of human and financial resources available The list below illustrates the choice of promotional tools available to port management which is intent on promoting the port or a specific service:

- Website
  In recent years the worldwide web has become the means for promotion of a company. World ports make wide use of this communication channel and great effort to ensure that the information meets the needs of its customers and other interested parties. A well designed website with simple user navigation enables appropriate information to made easily available. In addition to information concerning the port, there is ample opportunity to provide links to other port service providers.

- Advertising
  Advertising costs money. Advertising is used for different purposes, to promote a new service, to reinforce present activities or to create general awareness. Choosing the message and the media by which the message will be projected within a limited budget is a challenge. Evaluating the effectiveness of advertising spend is difficult. Advertising opportunities are many and include billboards, newspapers, cinema, television and industrial journals. Ports tend to be market specific and focussed in their advertising.

- Direct Mailing
  Direct mailing using an established data base of interested parties can be cost effective. The development of a database including the identification of customers and their addresses, the choice and personalisation of the message and the methods of mailing, electronic or traditional need to be considered. The evaluation of the effectiveness of this form of promotion is important.

  An issue to be considered in all communications is the maintenance and updating of the database. To be effective considerable administrative costs have to be allocated to this area.

- International Exhibitions and Fairs
  Presence at exhibitions can be a positive form of promotion. Selecting the exhibition or fair to attend is important as it will define the interest group attending. Many exhibitions are linked with conferences aimed at specific interest groups. Fairs are more generic in nature but often provide the opportunity for short presentations and seminars. There is a cost to exhibition attendance including design, construction, location and size of the stand. In addition transport costs, manning costs, follow up and evaluation costs have to be considered when deciding to exhibit. Conference organisers may alternate the exhibition location to widen the scope of the market. A good example of this is the bi-annual Pulp and Paper Industries (PPI) exhibition and conference which alternates between Europe and North America.

- Port Open Days
  To promote itself a port may decide to organise its own Port Open Day. Choosing how this can be undertaken without interfering with the 24/7 operational activities of the port needs careful consideration. Port Open Days may be limited to a specific area of the port and usually for a specific purpose. Safety and security of the public is a major concern.

- Educational Facilities
  Many major ports provide educational facilities allowing school, college and university students access to the port. Permanent exhibitions regarding the activities of the port, the opportunity for guided port tours and the provision of information can be integrated into a single student package. There are excellent examples of this form of promotion in European ports.

7.1.13   Other Tools

In addition to the above there are many other promotional tools available, some of which may be incorporated within those already mentioned, but all of which can be used separately. Other tools include, personal selling, direct business trips, use of representatives, networking, directory listing, conference organisation, attendance and participation, quality brochures and press advertorial.

7.2   CONCLUSION

Competition in the port sector is complex and has multiple facets depending on the nature, scope and scale of the port activity.

Based on a detailed analysis of a port's internal and external environment, a marketing strategy can be designed and developed to meet the competition. The marketing strategy will include a coherent and costed plan for the promotion of the port.

The task of port marketing starts with data collection, information analysis, and market research. It ends with strategy formulation and the implementation of a marketing plan using a mix of different marketing tools which are available, of which promotion is the most evident.

Feedback and regular evaluation of the marketing plan is important as this will inform port management about the effectiveness of the marketing effort.

7.3   SELF-ASSESSMENT AND TEST QUESTIONS

Attempt the following and check your answers from the text.

1. What are the substantive areas of information required by port managers in order to inform them of their position within the market place?

2. What do you understand by market segmentation and what is its relevance to the market research effort of a port?

3. Compare and contrast the use of printed media and the world-wide web for promoting the services of a port.

4. If you were to design a port website from scratch list a hierarchy of information you would display. For each hierarchial level give reasons for your choice. (To answer this question it might be helpful to study a live port website)

Having completed Chapter Seven attempt the following and submit your essay to your Tutor.

1. Port and port services operates in a dynamic global environment.

    State and examine what you consider will be the dominant marketing challenges facing port management during the next decade.

2. You have taken on the role as Marketing Director of a new general purpose terminal built in a developing economy. The terminal is able to handle container, RO RO and break bulk ships. The local economy is based on the production of cash crops and primary materials. It imports consumer goods from overseas. The objective of building the port in the area is to help support economic development of the hinterland.

    Discuss the techniques, promotion tools and the features of a marketing plan which will help the port achieve its objectives.

Chapter 8

PORT PLANNING

8.1   INTRODUCTION

Port Planning is a critical task of management and is undertaken to achieve optimum use of the present resources available and those that may be made available in the future. Investment needs in resources, particularly infrastructure and capital equipment is costly and requires long term commitment.

There are four types of planning process associated with ports, namely Operational Planning, Annual Planning, Medium-term Planning and Long-term (Master) Planning:

- **Operational Planning** is associated with the allocation of facilities and equipment for daily/short-term activities and includes berth allocation, ship and quay transfer operations.

- **Annual Planning** is associated with budgeting for the next annual round of resource allocation. It is an annual financial planning task by which revenues and expenditures are reviewed and adjusted to potential changes in income, expenditure and profit. Annual planning should not be confused with the financial planning of port projects, which is an integrated part of either medium-term or long-term planning.

- **Medium-term Planning** concerns a multi-year port plan, normally between three and five years, in which there is a strategic orientation to the port market and the port corporation. The combination of market planning and corporate planning is usually referred to as **strategic port planning**.

- **Long-term or Master Planning** concerns an extensive time period, which can be several decades in length. Long-term planning involves the development of new infrastructure facilities, such as terminals, warehouses and road networks. It also includes the acquisition of large mechanical handling equipment, for example gantry cranes and yard equipment which have a useful life span extending beyond ten years.

Annual planning follows the tasks described in Chapter Four on Port Finance. Long-term or Master Planning is a considerable task which involves parties beyond those who have an immediate interest in the port operations, including politicians, city planners and environmentalists. It is therefore beyond the scope of this book. Chapter Eight will therefore deal with **port planning at the operational and strategic level**.

Types of Planning \ Description	Time Horizon	Tasks	Actors
Operational	Daily or weekly	Short-term allocations of resources to daily/weekly activities.	Operational managers: harbour master, yard manager, warehouse manager.
Annual	Yearly	Annual budgeting of revenues and expenditures.	Almost everybody from operational managers, departmental managers to port directors.
Medium-term (Strategic Port Planning)	3 to 5 years	Allocation of existing resources and those to be acquired in the medium-run to existing and anticipated activities in line with traffic forecasts.	A team of strategic managers from each department e.g. marketing, HR, financial.
Long-term (Master)	10 years or more	Planning of port development such as in terms of new or large infrastructure facilities, long-life span superstructure/equipment.	Senior port managers, regional/central governments, community members (environmental groups and agencies, city planners, local residents).

Table 8.1 – Comparison of the Different Levels of Port Planning

8.1.1   Operational Planning

Traditional textbooks limit port operational planning to meeting the daily demands of ships, from their arrival in port, until departure. They tend to focus on the resource and allocations required for effective ship operation and cargo handling performance on the berth.

With the development of intermodal and logistics systems, port operational planning is now required to consider cargo flow management at both the inland interface as well as at the seaport terminal. Port operations' managers need to have an understanding of the planning processes which ensure the efficient and integrated flow of vehicles and cargo-transfer methods.

Operational planning can be divided into two main activities, information management and resource allocation.

1. **Information management** refers to the collection and analysis of data and information regarding ship and cargo arrival at the seaport terminal. Physical and technical information regarding the ship and cargo is required in addition to the organisational arrangements for their handling.

2. **Resource allocation** follows information management. It is concerned with the planning of berth allocation, which on common user berths is normally established on a first-come first-served basis. Resource allocation also has to consider the availability of the port workforce, mechanical handling equipment, transport and support infrastructure. The planning of intermodal operations, including receipt and delivery of cargo follows the same procedures but may involve other sets of problems such as congestion or transit delays which are outside the immediate control of the port.

8.1.2   Planning Elements

Operational planning includes the following elements:

- Berth planning

- Loading and unloading planning

- Yard planning

- Intermodal operations planning

- Performance monitoring

8.1.3 Berth Planning

Berth Planning requires a knowledge of berth configuration, including length, available draught alongside and capacity. It also needs information about each individual ship such as its length, service pattern, Estimated Time of Arrival (ETA) and Estimated Time of Departure (ETD). Constraints may be imposed by arrival and departure draughts and associated tidal conditions. Information is necessary to plan and allocate the appropriate berth for each expected ship.

Berthing ships can meet with pilotage difficulties, including manoeuvrability at slow speed, local currents and the effect of wind.

8.1.4 Loading and Unloading Planning

Planning the loading and unloading of a ship requires information concerning cargo, ship structure and available port resources, including manpower and cargo handling equipment.

Cargo data can be generally found in the ship's Manifest and the Stowage Plan. The ship's Manifest is a listing of the cargo loaded on the ship The Stowage Plan is a working document which describes the space allotted to specific cargo.

Information regarding the ship is found in the ship's specification. Ship's data which is of interest to the operational planner are the number of hatches, hold capacities, hatchway dimensions, types and Safe Working Loads (SWL) of onboard handling equipment. Technical features of each vessel also need to be known and include ship stability and for large ships structural strength limitations. Knowledge of the disposition and quantity of fuel oil and ballast water carried to trim the ship, is of importance.

Planning the allocation of port resources is in part determined by the turnaround demand by the ship operator. In planning resources, consideration will have to be given to the availability of workforce, cargo handling equipment, warehousing and transport needs for each expected ship.

Planning the loading and unloading element needs to identify the amount and type of cargo to be handled and assigns to it the right combination of operational resources in the most efficient way.

Compared to general purpose ship operations, the handling of standard size containers at the seaport terminal allows an operator to consider the use of Operational Research (OR) techniques, including optimisation and queuing theory, to achieve efficient use of resources. The identification of each container is critical to the activity and is achieved by providing a unique numeric identifier. To trace the container in the port and onboard the ship numeric location identification is also used. Further information needs include destination port, gross weight, container size and special needs associated with refrigerated commodities, out of gauge cargoes and dangerous goods.

8.1.5 Yard Planning

Yard planning concerns the planning of the seaport terminal configuration and layout. It has to take into account storage and warehousing needs and allow for vehicle movements along defined pathways.

Container yard planning needs to consider the location and relocation for containers by status, ship assignment, import, export or transhipment. Planning will take into account the flexibility and constraints of the yard system employed, that is straddle carrier operation, gantry system, front end loaders or tractor chassis combinations. A knowledge of container stack height limitations, separation of special containers and the need for entry and exit processing will have an impact on yard planning. Yard planning will also need to consider container transfer to and from other transport systems including road, rail, barge and feeder shipping.

8.1.6 Intermodal System Planning

Intermodal system planning takes place at the inland interface and has similar demands to berth planning. It includes freight configuration, arrival and departure control, loading and unloading planning for road, rail and barge transport. Much of the planning challenges at this level relates to the choice between direct routing and indirect routing to the seaport terminal. The need for a functional transfer system supported by correct documentation and clearance is important.

8.1.7 Performance Monitoring

Performance monitoring allows a continuous review-process of operational activity in order to plan future activities. Performance monitoring is undertaken by analysing four main performance indicators, namely; output, service utilisation, productivity and efficiency, at each process stage. The details for the calculation of these indicators are depicted in the Chapter on port management.

8.1.8 Queuing Theory and the Problem of Berth Assignment and Port Capacity

One of the most frequent problems faced by port managers is the availability of sufficient berths to accommodate every ship calling at the port without causing serious delays or increasing the waiting time.

The problem is due to the combination of two major factors:

1.   The random pattern of arrival of ships at the port

2.   The limited number of berths at the port (port capacity)

The problem is not unique. A supermarket manager has to solve a similar problem with the random pattern of shopper arriving at the payment gate and a limited number of payment gates. The supermarket manager will wish to minimise the number of open gates so that his limited staff can be deployed undertaking other tasks such as shelf filling. To ensure shopper satisfaction long queues are not acceptable as there is the risk of losing customers to more efficiently managed supermarkets. The ideal is to establish a formula whereby a critical level of customer queuing, for example ten persons in a queue, will necessitate opening an additional payment gate. In sustained busy situations it may be necessary to invest in new payment gates. The solution is a compromise between the cost of customers waiting time (satisfaction) and the cost of operating a payment gate or opening an extra one. Figure 8.1 illustrates the port problem related to establishing optimum port capacity.

The major problem faced in short-term port planning is that the ships' arrival pattern and the precise arrival times are difficult to estimate. The limited number of available berths compounds the difficulty creating a queuing problem which is more complex to manage than the one referred to in the supermarket example.

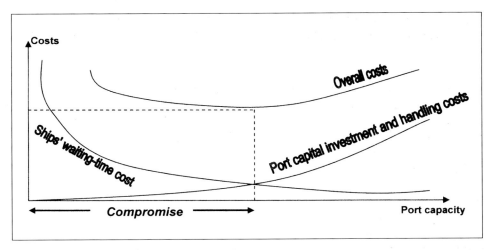

Figure 8.1 – Illustration of the Interaction Between Port Capacity and Ships' Time in Port

The maximum berth occupancy ratio (or e critical level) depends on the number of berths available and the arrival pattern of ships. A ratio has been computed statistically by United Nations Conference for Trade and Development (UNCTAD) for random vessel arrivals. Table 8.2 provides maximum occupancy ratios by number of berths for liner shipping. At the inland port gate the queuing problem is simpler to predict and solve as inland transport system works generally on a just-in-time basis.

Number of berths	Max occupancy ratio
1	30%
2	50%
3	60%
4	66%
5	70%
6	74%
7	77%
8	78%

Table 8.2 – Occupancy Ratios for Liner Ships (Source: UNCTAD)

The relationship between the waiting-time of a ship due to non-available berths and the service time when the ship is on the berth (which includes both working and non-working periods) is called the **waiting-time factor**. In berth planning it is important to give priority to regular time/day or week services over irregular berth allocation service requests. The system should be sufficiently flexible to cope with changes to a ships' arrival and departure schedule.

8.1.9 Methods and Estimates of Port Capacity

The physical constraints of ports are the number and capacity of berths, sheds, open storage areas and handling systems. Each factor has an influence in the performances of the others:

- the handling productivity determines the berthing time of the ship and consequently the berth occupancy ratio and the waiting time.

- the capacity of the yard and the design of the layout influence the handling productivity.

- administrative delays (e.g. customs clearance) and other bottlenecks determine the dwell time of the cargo, hence the transit and storage-yard space needed.

8.1.10 Berth capacity

To estimate the capacity of a berth, an analysis of ratios associated with handling rates are analysed from which maximum output is computed.

tonnes/ship-worked hour = tonnes/gang-hour x average number of gangs/ship

tonnes/service hour = tonnes/ship-worked hour x worked hour/service time

Annual Maximum Berth Capacity = tonnes/service hour x 24hrs x 365 days x maximum occupancy ratio x number of berths

---

Berth Capacity – Example

Calculate the Annual Maximum Berth Capacity of a general cargo terminal with four berths, given the following:

Tonnes/gang hour	25 tonnes:
Number of gangs per ship	2.5:
Worked time/service time	45%:
Maximum berth occupancy ratio	44% (see Table 8.2)

Working

Tonnes/ship worked hour = 62.5 tonnes (25 x 2.5)

Tonnes/service hour = 28.13 tons (62.5 x 0.45)

Solution

Annual Maximum Berth Capacity = 28.13 x 24 x 365 x 0.66 x 4 = 650,000 tonnes

Changing the inputs, the Annual Maximum Berth Capacity can be altered.

Simulation using Excel spreadsheets or special software packages can be helpful in providing solutions to varied inputs.

Cargo-type and packing methods influence a berth's capacity. Table 8.3 shows typical gang-output levels for various types of cargo-packing. It also illustrates efficiency improvements created by the unitisation of cargo.

Type of packing	Gang output (tonnes/gang-hour)
Cases and boxes	12 - 15
Bags	20 - 25
Pre-slung bags	40 - 50
Pallets	25 - 40
Containerised cargo: shore gantry ship crane	200 - 250 120 - 150
RO RO	300 - 500
Dry bulk	1,000

(World Bank and UNCTAD)

Table 8.3 – Typical Gang-output Levels Compiled from Different Sources

8.1.11 Storage Capacity

Storage capacity in a port area is often limited by port-city interface issues, physical features and environmental concerns. Land expansion is expensive and ports attempt to optimise their operations on the basis of existing land facilities. Storage capacity depends on two main factors, dwell time and cargo type.

1. **Dwell time** is defined as the time in days and hours that cargo occupies space on the yard or in the shed.

2. **Cargo type**: Individual cargo types have their own characteristics in terms of storage capacity needed. Stowage factor is a measure of volume occupied by one tonne of goods and is given for each commodity in cubic metres per tonne, or traditionally cubic feet per ton. There is a cost to storage which is volume related. The relationship between the cargo Stowage Factor and the floor area required for storage will depend upon stack height. The use of shelving in modern warehouses permits increased use of floor space.

Storage Capacity (cubic metres)

$$\text{Storage Capacity} = \frac{\text{tonnes throughput per year} \times \text{Stowage Factor} \times \text{Dwell time}}{365}$$

Tonnage throughput per year (theoretical)

$$\text{Tonnes throughput per year} = \frac{\text{Storage Capacity} \times 365}{\text{Stowage Factor} \times \text{Dwell time}}$$

8.1.12 Port Congestion

Comparing traffic forecasts and the maximum capacity of port facilities will provide an assessment about the likely occurrence of congestion either at the berth or within storage. Congestion problems can be solved by one or the combination of the following actions:

In the short term congestion can be reduced by:

- extending the port hours of working,

- changing the method of working e.g. increased use of operational resources

- providing incentives for workers e.g. additional payments

- accelerating customs clearance

- limiting the dwell time of cargo in port,

In the long term congestion can be reduced by:

- purchasing new equipment

- building new berths

- creating additional storage space

At an operational level, the focus should be on optimising the output of existing facilities. Table 8.4 is a spread sheet simulation exercise that illustrates how improvements in efficiency can have impact on increasing port capacity.

ESTIMATE OF THE MAXIMUM CAPACITY OF A PORT				
Ratios	General-cargo terminal		Container-terminal	
	Simulation	Current situation	Simulation	Current situation
Tonnes (or TEU)/gang hour	25	20	25	17
Average number of gangs/ship	2.5	2.5	2.5	3
Tonnes (or TEU)/ship-worked hour	**62.5**	**50**	**62.5**	**51**
Worked time/service time	45%	45%	45%	45%
Tonnes/ship-service hour	**28.125**	**22.5**	**28.125**	**22.95**
Max occupancy ratio	66%	66%	50%	50%
Annual available hours	8760	8760	8760	8760
Number of berths	4	4	2	2
Max. Capacity	**650,430**	**520,344**	**246,375**	**201,042**
Capacity per berth (in tonnes or TEU)	162,608	130,086	123,188	100,521

Table 8.4 – Increase of Potential Maximum Port Capacity Due Improvements in Port Efficiency

8.1.13   Strategic Port Planning

Having considered Operational Planning the next planning stage considered in the Chapter is Medium-Term Planning, more commonly known as **Strategic Planning**.

Strategic Planning involves the preparation of a formal document, which identifies the organisation's long-term mission, formulates its medium-term objectives and strategies, and guides the implementation of such strategies through detailed business plans, and a regular annual review. As such strategic planning is linked to both long-term planning and annual planning, but differs from them by its medium-term time horizon, its strategic focus, and its level of decision-making.

Strategic plans are prepared with a three to five year horizon but will be reviewed on an annual basis. Whilst a strategic plan may include a limited amount of capital investment its primary focus is on the use of its existing resources of finance, physical structure and human input. A changing competitive market can impact on port resource allocation.

The process of strategic planning begins with the formulation of a set of medium-term objectives and an understanding of possible internal and external changes that may impact on the port. The use of market trend forecasts will help port management appreciate the continuing attractiveness, or otherwise, of the port.

Undertaking a review of the port's strengths and weaknesses by a SWOT analysis will help port management identify and select the proper strategies needed to achieve previously stated objectives. In light of forecasts and analysis it may be necessary to adjust present objectives.

A typical framework for Strategic Port Planning is shown in Figure 8.2. The process commences and concludes with the setting of objectives. Objectives are set at three levels:

1.   Long Term – corresponding to the mission statement set at the corporate level,

2.   Medium Term – corresponding to the strategic plan objectives set at the departmental level,

3.   Short Term – corresponding to targets, sometimes known as sub-objectives set at the level of the unit.

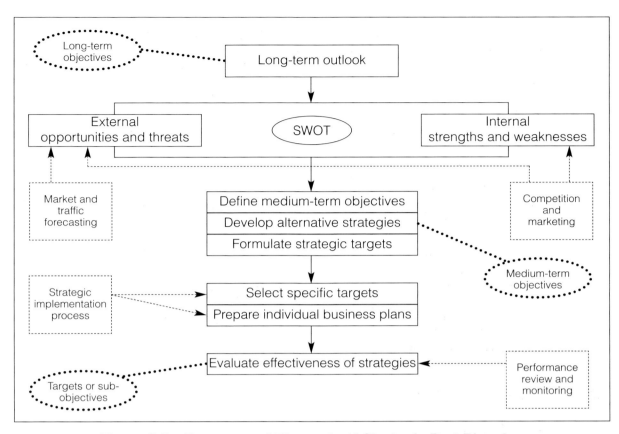

Figure 8.2 – Process and Elements of Strategic Port Planning

In strategic planning, the emphasis is on medium-term objectives which should be formulated in respect of the port's mission statement (long-term planning) and broken-down into short-term targets. Examples of medium-term objectives could include a stated reduction of ship waiting time, an increase of container throughput, or the introduction of new arrangements for resource reallocation. (for example the introduction of a 24-hour working pattern for container terminals).

Four elements required by a **Strategic Port Planning** process are:

1. Port traffic forecasting,

2. Port competition and marketing,

3. Strategic implementation process,

4. Performance review.

Port competition, marketing and performance review are covered elsewhere and therefore discussion is limited to aspects of port traffic forecasting and the implementation process of strategic plans.

8.1.14 Port Traffic Forecasting

The essence of port traffic forecasting is to establish the:

- type and tonnage of cargo that will likely move through the port,

- packaging form of such commodities,

- ships including tonnage and frequency of call,

- inland transport vehicle types.

Traffic forecasting requires a combination of commercial and economic knowledge, and a good understanding of different forecasting techniques, including statistics and relevant software packages.

Traffic forecasting is linked to market research. It requires the collection and analysis of data about:

- cargo origin and destination,

- production, consumption, and distribution patterns,

- evolution of the volume and nature of trade in the region,

- freight transport decisions (e.g. shipping routes, inland transport networks),

- intermodal arrangements, including the establishment of distribution centres,

- competitors current and expected traffic,

- performance and costs of the port vis-à-vis its competitors,

- competitors' strategies and investment plans,

- changes in public policy, including competition and environmental regulations.

Usually, traffic forecasting is undertaken through time series analysis using extrapolation techniques to work out a future general trend line. In addition to the general trend, the following factors need to be considered.

- **Seasonal factors**

  Seasonal factors are regular fluctuations which take place within one complete period of time. The period is usually of an annual nature and will reflect harvesting times for agricultural produce or peak times for consumer goods such as Christmas. On a shorter time scale daily fluctuations may be observed in patterns of ship calls where for example a shipping line calling at a particular port .may have no ship calls on Saturday but five ships on Monday.

- **Cyclical factors**

  Cyclical factors concern longer term of fluctuation which may take several years to complete. The economic cycle of stagnation, recession and expansion is likely to have an important and lasting impact on port traffic.

- **Random Factors**

  Random Factors are non-predictable and short term including events such as a dock strike or pollution incidents that may have an immediate impact on traffic levels.

8.1.15   Strategic Implementation Process

Alternative strategies for implementing a port's strategic plan need to be identified and selected during the process of objective-strategy formulation. They can be clustered into two main categories. The first category is known as an offensive strategy which attempts to consolidate and increase the port's traffic and market share. The second category is the defensive strategy which seeks to counter or minimise negative impacts on port's market share and competitiveness.

Once the strategy has been identified it will be implemented through the business plan. The business plan will detail appropriate assignments at the different level of port operational management. The development of a business plan will be undertaken under the direction of top management, and will be co-ordinated by a designated senior manager. A typical business plan will include the following:

- the main objectives of the business,

- a series of actions to be undertaken,

- detailed job assignments,

- inventory of resources and their allocation,

- detailed budgets and financial projections,

- specific programme targets,

- management structure,

- performance monitoring and evaluation processes.

Performance monitoring and evaluation processes are continuous and may establish a mismatch between planned and actual targets. If appropriate, corrective action may be needed. Financial reporting and budget planning are the two critical areas to be monitored. When a mismatch has been identified major corrections will be taken to meet the new situation either though a modification of the strategy, or a change to the business action plan. A system of performance monitoring, with specific indicators will require development in order to ensure fair comparison and ensure credibility of the monitoring process.

8.1.16   Towards an Integrated System for Port Operational and Strategic Planning

As mentioned at the beginning of Chapter Eight, different elements and levels of port planning need to be integrated to ensure achievement of both short-term and long-term objectives. Port management is involved in a variety of planning activities which are intended to optimise the port's resources and improve the satisfaction of the port customer and user. All planning schemes must be undertaken jointly and not in isolation, since the success of each planning activity is dependent on the performance of the other. Figure 8.3 proposes an integrated framework for port planning, with a focus on port capacity, optimal utilisation and the allocation of port resources.

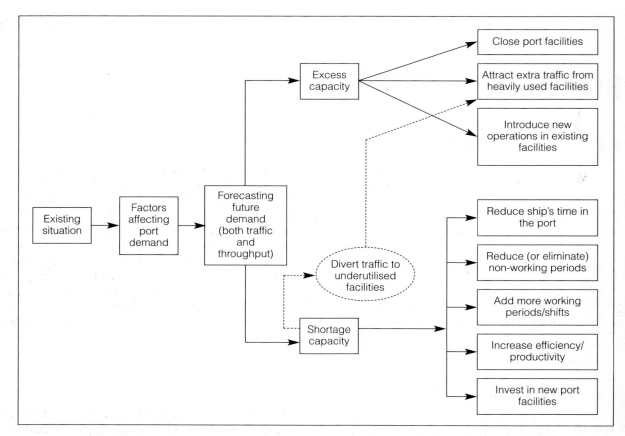

Figure 8.3: An Integrated Approach for Port Planning and Development

8.2   SELF-ASSESSMENT AND TEST QUESTIONS

Attempt the following and check your answers from the text.

1.   Operational port planning has five elements. For a port with which you are familiar consider any THREE areas and write a brief report on each.

2.   Critically discuss the methods which can be used to reduce port congestion in the short term.

3.   An estimate of the maximum capacity for a **Container Terminal** is shown in Table 4. Study the table and comment on the variance between the current and simulated results.

4,   What is a SWOT analysis? Describe how a SWOT analysis is used in the strategic port planning process.

5.   State the purpose of a Port Traffic Forecast and the use to which it is put. Comment on the factors which may distort any general trends.

6.   Figure 8.4 shows an integrated approach to port planning and development. Describe in words what is shown and discuss the management issues which arise when a shortage of capacity is forecast.

Having completed Chapter Eight attempt **ONE** of the following and submit your essay to your Tutor.

1.   Port Planning is undertaken at different levels. Describe why this is required, comment on the planning issues associated at each level and explain how integration of planning activities can be co-ordinated by port management.

OR

2.   For a port of your choice write a report on **either** the operational planning process **or** the strategic planning process. In your report critically analyse the effectiveness of the processes involved.

Chapter 9

PORT EQUIPMENT

9.1   INTRODUCTION

Chapter Nine provides an overview of the equipment used by the ports industry for the interchange of cargo between ship and shore. It will consider equipment used for the movement and storage at the port terminal for general cargo, unitised cargo, dry bulk cargo and liquid bulk cargo. It will cover support activities required of the port terminal for efficient operations. It has been noted in Chapter Two that cargo characteristics have an impact on carriage requirements. Similarly a knowledge of cargo characteristics is necessary to appreciate how goods can be safely handled and stored in the port terminal environment. The shipowner demands fast turnaround of his ship. The port operator responds by providing the equipment which best meet the need. Port equipment is constantly being developed to provide optimum handling efficiency at the port terminal. The principles of cargo operation in which the port operator has a clear interest concern three areas: the safety of the cargo, the safety of the ship and above all the safety of people.

9.2   TERMINAL ARRANGEMENTS

Terminals need to be able to provide the facility for cargo interchange between transport modes and appropriate storage facilities. Land area available will be a major influence in the operational design of the terminal yard and will influence the type of port equipment needed. Storage facilities may be provided by warehousing for general cargo, open yards for containers, open space or silos for dry bulk cargoes and tanks for liquid bulk cargoes. Two main forms of storage required at the port interface are 'transit storage' and 'warehouse storage'.

The Chapter will look at the operational features of:

1.   General purpose (cargo) terminals,

2.   Unitised cargo terminals

    (i)   Container

    (ii)   RO RO

    (iii)   Pallet

3.   Bulk Terminals

    (i)   Dry Bulk

    (ii)   Liquid Bulk

Each terminal is different in detail but the following common features are present: and will be covered:

A.   Ship/shore interchange equipment,

B.   Yard equipment,

C.   Yard layout,

D.   Yard control and administration.

9.3 GENERAL PURPOSE (CARGO) TERMINAL

Introduction

Ship to shore and shore to ship transfer general cargo operations can be found in most ports of the world, despite the development of untisation and carriage of bulk cargoes. General cargo operations entails the break of bulk such that individual pieces can be individually handled. General cargo is consolidated at the ship's side prior to loading and broken into individual units at the ship's side when discharged. The principle Lift-On Lift-Off (LO LO) equipment is either the ship's cranes or derricks or the port quayside cranes. Sometimes a combination of both ship and shore based cranes are used. Stevedoring equipment which allows for the consolidation of the individual pieces is basic and determined by the characteristics of the cargo type. Sufficient manpower is required for the operation and safety is of great importance.

9.3.1 Ship-Shore Interchange Equipment

Slewing Jib Cranes

Quayside cargo handling slewing jib cranes are designed to handle general cargo. They are able to lift loads of between 3 and 10 tonnes. The component parts include a pedestal, jib and driver's cab. The crane is designed to move on a rail track along the length of the quay permitting positioning. Quayside cranes have the ability to 'spot' position the cargo by luffing and slewing the jib. A hoisting winch allows the vertical movement of the crane hook which is attached to the hoisting cable. A quayside crane will undertake 12 to 20 cycles per hour.

Mobile Harbour Cranes

Many ports now invest in mobile harbour cranes which are versatile and allow for flexible positioning within the port. They are built to undertake many tasks in port by being equipped with appropriate lifting gear, e.g. spreaders and grabs. The crane is controlled from a tower cab, whose position on the tower allows the whole operational area to be viewed. Crane manufacturers produce a series of mobile cranes with lifting capacity ranging from 6 tonnes to 120 tonnes and a jib operational radius of between 8 and 56 metres.

Stevedoring Equipment

Stevedoring equipment describes the equipment necessary to sling different cargoes. For general cargo, slings utilise rope, wire or chain, either used singly or in combination for specialised cargoes. Use of inappropriate slings can result in damage to cargo.

9.3.2 General Cargo Shore Storage

General cargo is stored in port areas for consolidation prior to loading or storage after discharge. Warehouses are a part of the general cargo port scene, but containerisation and 'just in time' transport methods have reduced demand in port areas. Warehouses are used for long term storage of specialised cargoes, for example; fertiliser, tobacco and fruit. Short term general cargo storage makes use of transit sheds.

Warehouses

For long term storage many cargoes require specialist care. The specialist warehouse will be constructed for a specific cargo with known characteristics. Maximum use of the warehouse volume is important. This can be achieved by the use of racking systems which permit a vertical stow of the cargo and the access by fork-lift trucks. Some cargoes e.g. tobacco and fruit, will need the warehouse to be temperature and humidity controlled. A secure environment is important for all cargoes, but specially for those which attract high levels of excise duty e.g. whisky. Other warehouse types may provide the opportunity for bagging and palletisation of bulk cargo e.g. plastic pallets.

Transit Shed

Transit sheds are used for the consolidation of break-bulk cargoes. They provide protection and security for the cargo. Transit sheds today are single storey buildings. Large roof spans eliminate the need for internal pillars, thus maximising the usable floor area. Wide doors to the terminal yard and quayside provide easy access for mechanical handling equipment e.g. fork-lift trucks, whilst recessed loading and unloading bays create easy transfer to and from road transport vehicles. Further consideration in transit warehouse design includes good lighting, adequate ventilation, good quality flooring and office accommodation located above the operational level. The floor area of the transit warehouse may be used to consolidate and separate specific cargoes by destination or type. A transit shed will not normally use racking systems for vertical storage due to the short-term stay of the cargo.

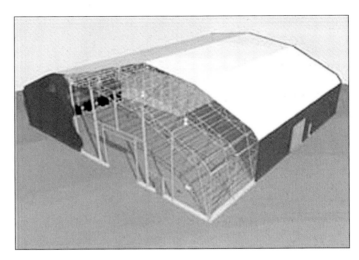

Figure 9.1 – A Modern Transit Shed – Rubb Building

9.4   UNITISED CARGO TERMINALS

The advent of unitisation caused a revolution in port operations. The traditional manual handling of general cargoes gave way to the use of sophisticated mechanical handling equipment for the transfer and movement of the freight container, pallet and RO RO cargoes.

9.5   CONTAINER TERMINAL EQUIPMENT

Equipment on a container terminal is required to lift-on and lift-off containers between the ship and shore. Further equipment is required to position containers into either the export/import area and retrieve them for delivery. Port equipment choice will vary depending on the yard area, frequency of ship calls, size of ship, capital available for investment, the flexibility of service required and the predicted containers throughput of the terminal. The types of equipment available include the ship shore quayside gantry, rail mounted or rubber tyred yard gantry cranes, terminal tractors and trailers, straddle carriers and interchangeable handling systems based on the fork lift truck. Automatic guided vehicles and automated gantries are used at certain terminals.

9.5.1   Ship-Shore Interchange Equipment

The **Quayside container gantry** is the most expensive piece of equipment required for lifting containers between ship and shore. The origins of the design can be traced back to gantries used for the handling of dry bulk cargoes such as iron ore and coal. The quayside container gantry consists four legs connected by cross beams capable of travelling along quayside rails. The legs support a raisable boom, which has outreach (over the quay edge) and backreach (over the container yard).

(Photo P Wright)

Figure 9.2 – A Quayside Container Gantry – Port of Antwerp

In the boomed out position, the boom provides a horizontal track for the movement of a trolley which supports the drivers cab and lifting mechanism. The lifting mechanism is linked through a head block to a container spreader. The single container spreader is normally of a telescopic type, capable of lifting standard ISO container types. The distance between the quayside legs and yard legs is known as the rail span. The quayside container gantry is electrically powered with power normally taken from the local electrical grid. The size of a quayside container gantry has increased with the development of the container ship. Modern quayside container gantries are required to span the width of the post panamax generation container ships (22 rows) and have a height necessary for associated vertical lifts (7 container tiers on deck). Container gantries are now being built capable of twin container lifts and may have a Safe Working Load (SWL) in excess of 80 tonnes. The operation of the quayside gantry is critical to the turn around of the container ship and establishing the port efficiency. In operation, sixty cycles per hour can be achieved. The critical specifications of a container gantry are its outreach, span between legs, backreach, hoisting speed and trolley travel speed. The **Mobile Harbour Crane** is often used at container terminals which have a limited throughput.

Figure 9.3 – The Mobile Harbour Crane

The lifting cycle and hence the rate of load and discharge of the mobile harbour crane is slower than that of the specialised quayside gantry crane. However its relatively low cost and greater flexibility of use for non-containerised cargo handling means it finds favour in smaller ports.

9.5.2   Yard Equipment – Containers

There are four common container yard systems.

1. Tractor and Chassis,

2. Straddle Carrier,

3. Yard Gantry Crane,

4. Front End Loader or Fork-Lift.

9.5.3   Tractor and Chassis Yard System

The tractor and chassis system is the simplest of all yard systems. A trailer chassis, pulled by a tractor unit, enables containers to be moved to and away from the quayside container gantry. The trailer chassis is stored in the container yard prior to or after delivery by the shipper. The chassis is equipped with locking devices to ensure the container can be secured for road haulage. Use of the skeletal trailer was very effective during the early days of containerisation when container numbers and pressure on land resources were limited. A full skeletal trailer system is rarely used today.

9.5.4   The Straddle Carrier

Figure 9.4 – The Straddle Carrier

The straddle carrier is a complex transfer vehicle specially designed for the movement of freight containers within a container terminal. It is used to service the quayside ship-shore gantry crane, stack containers in the terminal, often three high and transport one over two. It is used to load/unload road vehicles as well as select containers from the container stack. The straddle carrier is essentially a powered lifting frame capable of directional movement. It is equipped with a telescopic spreader between the legs of the frame capable of lifting loaded standard ISO container types, three tiers high. The straddle carrier is diesel powered and displaces its weight over four pairs of pneumatic tyres. An operator's cab is placed at the uppermost extremity of the vehicle. Radio and computer links between the operator and terminal control ensure that the straddle carrier is efficiently used. Critical specifications include: service weight (e.g. 60 tonnes), spreader capacity (SWL 40 tonnes), wheel loading (service weight + spreader capacity divided by the number of wheels), dimensions (including lift height and turning radius), travel speed (about 20 miles per hour) and spreader lift speed. Initial capital costs of a straddle carrier are high (about £300,000 per vehicle) and maintenance costs are also high. As the straddle carrier is specific to a port terminal, maintenance workshops will be required as part of the terminal facility.

9.5.5 Fork-Lift Truck

The fork-lift truck is a flexible sophisticated and expensive mechanical handling device. It is essentially a vehicle capable of lifting containers by a front end arrangement, which may be either bottom forks or a top lift spreader. Fork-lift trucks initially used in port work were small, capable of handing little in excess of 2 tonnes and preceded containerisation. Today, fork-lift trucks used in container terminals have a carrying capacity range between 28 and 50 tonnes and telescopic column extensions allowing a reach height of 13 metres. The specification of a fork-lift truck considers travel speed, lifting speed, climbing ability, fuel consumption, axle loading and mast height. The power unit for fork-lift trucks used in container operations is a diesel engine. Special attention in design is given to safety features including driver visibility and driver control systems.

Figure 9.5 – Fork-Lift Truck

Figure 9.6 – Reach Stacker

9.5.6 Front Loaders

Other specialist front end equipment used in container terminals in port areas, include the reach stacker and empty container hander. The **Reach Stacker** has an advantage over the fork-lift truck in being able to reach and stack three adjacent rows of containers. The fork-lift truck can only stack a single row. This allows greater flexibility in the storage and accessibility of containers. Stack heights are typically limited to 5 containers high the **Empty Container Handler** is used in yards dedicated to the storage of empty containers only. Of limited weight lifting capability (typically 8 tonnes SWL), the lifting devices can be used to service 8 high container stacks.

9.5.7 Rubber Tyred Gantry (RTG) and Rail Mounted Gantry (RMG)

Figure 9.7 – Rubber Tyred Gantry

Rubber tyred and rail mounted gantries are specialised pieces of container handling equipment which have high stacking capability. They vary in size, larger units allowing for four high container stacking and eight containers wide. They are used where there is high throughput and limited terminal area. The gantry structure supports a rail mounted horizontal trolley which spans the stacking area and adjacent road lane. Associated with the trolley is a control cab and lifting spreader.

Rubber Tyred Gantry (RTG) systems provide the facility for container stacking up to four high and 4 high and 5 containers wide. They are used for container terminals which have a medium to low throughput (up to 10,000 units per year) they are powered by diesel engines. The rubber tyred gantry offers flexibility of terminal layout without the necessity for permanent rail infrastructure.

The Rail Mounted Gantry (RMG) is used in port terminals which have high throughput. They will have a handling capacity of about thirty containers per hour. It is not unusual to have two or three rail mounted gantries occupying a crane runway which may have a length in excess of 700 metres. Rail mounted gantries can be fully automated.

9.5.8 Road Train

A road train consists of a tractor and a number of skeletal trailers which can be attached to each other allowing a train to be assembled of varied length. They are used where there is the need to move a number of containers about the container terminal.

9.5.9 Automatic Guided Vehicle (AGV)

In the ship operating zone of the container terminal some operators are using Automatic Guided Vehicles (AGV). Taking their positional information from an implanted grid, the AGVs deliver containers between the stacking area and the ship side. The vehicles are fully automatic and operate without drivers.

9.5.10 Container Spreaders

Common to all containers handling systems is the container spreader or lifting frame. The spreader has the length and width dimensions of the ISO freight containers. At each corner of the frame is a casting which incorporates a twist lock. The twistlock consists of a cam which can be rotated, manually or automatically and locks the lifting frame into the corner castings of the container, permitting vertical lift.

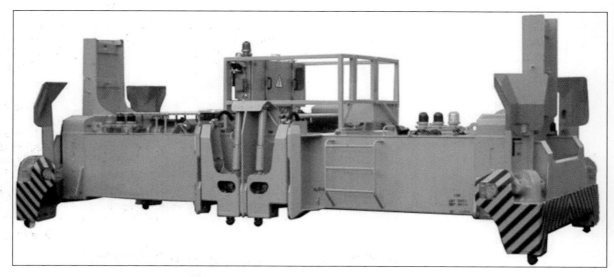

Figure 9.8 – A Quayside Container Gantry Spreader

There are a wide variation of container spreader types and that used depends upon the demand of the terminal. Container ship shore gantry cranes, straddle carriers and gantry systems all use automatic locking and telescopic spreaders which allows for efficient lifting and a rapid change capability when handling ISO standard containers. Container ship/shore gantry crane spreaders may have other facilities including twin-lift (or even four-lift) capability and spreader rotation. They will also incorporate flipper mechanisms at the spreader corners which help the gantry driver accurately locate the spreader onto the container allowing twistlock connection. Automatic spreaders are electro – hydraulically operated. The safe working load of a container ship-shore gantry crane spreader ranges between thirty and eighty tonnes.

9.5.11 Comparison of Container Yard Systems

No two container terminals are the same, but all have the same transfer needs. Whilst different mechanical handling equipment will be used, the overall layout remains common. The general layout has four operational zones extending landwards from the quayside. The zones are: the ship operating zone, the stacking zone for import and export cargoes, the zone for special containers (dangerous goods and refrigerated cargoes) and a zone for exchange and transfer of containers to and from land transport. Restrictions on equipment used are imposed by constraints, including boundaries and land area, container throughput, availability of finance and people skills. The table below provides a useful comparison of Container Yard Systems.

System Features	Tractor Chassis System	Straddle Carrier	Yard Gantry Crane System	Front-end Loader (FLT)
Land Utilisation (single tier)	**Very Poor** 185 TEU/hectare	**Good** 385 TEU/hectare	**Very Good** 750 TEU/hectare	**Poor** 275 TEU/hectare
Terminal Development Costs	**Very Low** High quality surface not necessary	**Medium** Hard wearing surface needed	**High** High loading bearing surface needed for crane wheels	**High** Heavy wear on terminal surface
Equipment Costs	**High** Number of chassis required	**Moderate** Six straddle carriers per ship/shore gantry	**High**	**Moderate** Cost effective for low throughputs
Equipment Maintenance Costs	Low	High	Low	Medium
Manning Levels 2 crane operation	**High** Low skills required	**Low** High Skills required	**High** Medium/High skills required	**Medium** Medium Skills required
Operating Factors	Good: accessibility Simple terminal organisation	High flexibility 2/3 stacking capability	Good land use scope for automation	Versatile

Source UNCTAD

Figure 9.9 – Container Yard Systems Comparison

9.5.12 Container Yard Control

Management of a container terminal is complex with many activities having to be coordinated effectively. A key to efficient operation is good terminal design and effective information transfer. The container terminal is a location where interchange of equipment and cargo takes place and liabilities transfer. At the Gate, the entry and exit point of the terminal, opportunity is provided for container inspections and the interchange of Equipment Reports. The Container Terminal is also a location where the nation state can measure its import and export activity and impose restrictions and/or impose duty/duties on cargoes moving across international boundaries. Customs authorities have an interest. Whilst the development of the container business has cut down petty theft, theft of individual containers can occur. Theft is largely preventable by secure control at the exit point. Independent facilities for dangerous goods, reefer containers and 'Out of Gauge' cargoes also have to be considered.

9.5.13 Container Yard Support

A container terminal is a facility which provides a package of activities and services to handle and control container flows from vessel to road, rail or water and *vice versa*. It is the physical link between the ocean and inland modes of transport and forms the major node of any containerised intermodal transport system. Facilities have to be provided at the terminal so that import and export containers can be received, containers can be stored, customs inspections can be facilitated, condition reports established and equipment repairs undertaken. Office space is also required by participants to the container terminal operation, including the ship's agents, container company or consortia representatives, ship and terminal planners and the terminal operator. Space will be required for terminal staff, including canteen and changing facilities. Central to a container terminal will be the control room, it will be fitted with radio and computer links allowing the terminal operator to effectively manage the interchange of containers, control the container yard, make effective use of wharf space and ensure optimum use of terminal handling equipment.

9.5.14 Container Freight Station

Also known as an Inland Container Depot the role of the Container Freight Station (CFS) is the consolidation of small break bulk cargoes for container stuffing and the forwarding of the container to the port for export. They also act as receiving station for Less than Container Loads (LCL). Container Freight Stations are located outside the container port and mainly some distance inland.

9.6 ROLL ON – ROLL OFF TERMINALS

The Roll On – Roll Off (RO-RO) system, if based on ship's equipment and self-driven road vehicles is the most simple of all cargo systems. At its most basic it requires little more from the port terminal than an appropriate length of quay. However, the simplistic ideal is rare and the loading and discharging of RO RO ships normally requires the use of additional handling equipment and manpower provided by the port terminal.

Tractor units will be needed to load or discharge unaccompanied road trailers. On longer routes, cargo may be loaded onto flatbed trailers requiring specialised (MAFI) tractors for the load/discharge operation.

Other cargo handling equipment required of the RO RO port terminal may include fork-lift trucks, reach stackers and top lifters.

Break bulk items if carried will require storage in transit sheds. The need to have sufficient drivers to ensure the smooth discharge of a RO RO vessel is a further concern. Roll On – Roll Off operations are totally dependent upon bridging the interface between ship and shore through the use of ship or shore based ramps.

9.6.1 Ramps

RO RO ships are equipped with their own ramp systems. Deep sea RO RO ships have quarter ramps or slewing quarter ramps which do not require a specialist port structure.

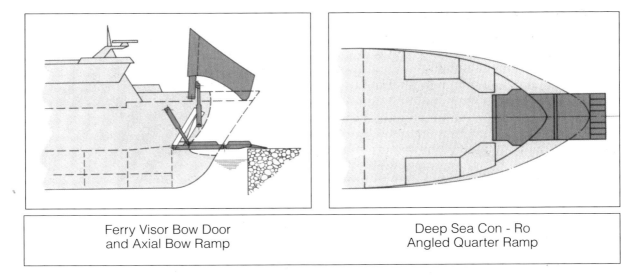

| Ferry Visor Bow Door and Axial Bow Ramp | Deep Sea Con - Ro Angled Quarter Ramp |

Figure 9.10 – Bow and Stern Ramp Systems

The left hand illustrations show a typical bow visor door and axial bow ramp commonly used on ferries. The ramp is an integral part of the ship and serves as a watertight bulkhead when in the stowed position.

The two illustrations on the right show an axial stern ramp of deep sea RO RO. The upper right illustration shows the axial stern ramp in the port mode. Three sections are visible. The lower right photograph shows the axial stern ramp in the stowed position for sailing.

The deep sea RO RO can lay alongside a suitable linear berth and cargo can be loaded and discharged ashore using its own two or three lane stern ramp. Ferries are normally equipped with fore and aft axial ramps and in the interests of rapid turnaround will depend on supporting port based equipment.

Where there is no tide, a shore fixed masonry arrangement for the ramp may be used. If the RO RO terminal is built where there are tidal conditions the incline the ramp makes with the shore will need to be considered so that vehicles will not ground or hit top edge during transfer. To overcome excessive inclines a bridge ramp or floating (pontoon) structure is used. The bridge ramp can be a complex and expensive structure and is frequently used on ferry terminals. It may have two deck access arrangements. The ramp is hinged at the shore point and the lead edge will move vertically to accommodate tidal change and change of ships draft. A floating pontoon will be linked to the shore by a ramp which has a length sufficient to ensure that its inclination will not cause difficulty for vehicles during loading and discharging operations. The axial ramp of the RO RO vessel will be placed onto the pontoon providing an effective connection.

9.6.2   RO RO Vehicles

A vehicle using a RO RO vessel may be presented either as driver accompanied or non-driver accompanied trailer cargo. The decision on how it is presented will depend on many factors including sea journey length, driver preference and hours legislation.

When presented as driver accompanied the port requirements are for shore parking allocation, booking and documentary service and driver recreation. When non-driver accompanied trailers are presented to the port it will be the responsibility of the port to load/ unload the ship. To do this the port will have specialised tractors, which can link with the trailer. The trailer can be towed or pushed from its shore storage position to the allocated slot on the vessel.

Figure 9.11 – A MAFI Tractor

Some cargo may not be presented by the shipper as RO RO cargo. In such cases it can be consolidated onto a non-road trailer eg, a MAFI trailer, for movement onto the vessel. Due to the rapid speed of loading and unloading, safety of personnel and security of cargo are two critical aspects of RO RO ship operation. The Maritime and Coastguard Agency (MCA) *Code of Safe Working Practice for Seamen* (1998) has valuable advice for all who load and discharge RO RO ships,

9.7   PALLET SYSTEMS

Pallets were at one time a very strong contender as a unit load system to the ISO freight container. On a certain number of trade routes, particularly those concerned with the movement of fruit they still provide a unitised system. The pallet system is composed of the pallet, the fork-lift truck, the ship-shore transfer equipment and appropriate warehouse storage.

9.7.1   Pallets

The dimensions and structure of standard pallets used in maritime operations have already been described (see Chapter Two). The standard pallet provides the core unit of a palletised system. To make the ship-shore transfer more efficient four or six pallets may be consolidated onto a pallet lift.

(Photo: P Wright)

Figure 9.12 – Pallet-lift and Fork-lift Trucks Used in the Transfer of Fruit Pallets

9.7.2 Fork-Lift Trucks

Standard diesel or gas powered fork-lift trucks with a 2-4 tonne telescopic single or double lifting front end arrangement are used as the main vehicle for the movement of pallets. For best use they require a good pavement surface on which to operate. Fork-lift trucks may be equipped with an onboard radio linked computer and scanning device to ensure the correct positioning of the pallet.

9.7.3 Ship-Shore Transfer Equipment

Transfer operations between ship and shore can be undertaken directly through the use of shore based fork-lift trucks and specialised ship types, or by fork-lift trucks used in combination with shore based general cargo slewing cranes.

When using the shore based slewing crane for the transfer of pallets it will be equipped with either a balanced fork-lift attachment or a set of wing pallet spreader bars. On specialized berths a pallet tray or frame arrangement capable of accommodating a set of four or six pallets may be used, Such an arrangement reduces turnaround time for the ship, allows rapid and flexible dispersal of cargo from the ships side and is competitive with other unit load methods including the container.

9.7.4 Warehousing and the Storage of Palletised Cargo

It is normal that palletised cargoes are stored in warehouses. The warehouse will be designed to ensure that the traffic flow of goods in and goods out is efficient. The roof will be largely self-supporting minimising the need for internal columns and pillars. Doors will be of full height and have a width compatible with the flow of traffic. Ground storage may be appropriate for some palletised cargoes, but warehouse design now often incorporates racks, ensuring the full internal volume can be utilised. Specialised warehouses may have bagging and pallet consolidation equipment incorporated into their design.

(Photo: P Wright)

Figure 9.13 – Warehouse pallet racking system

(Photo: P Wright)

Figure 9.14 –Warehouse bagging facility

9.8 DRY BULK CARGO TERMINALS

9.8.1 Terminal Equipment

Dry bulk terminal equipment is provided to transfer the commodity to and from storage to the ships. Dry bulk cargo handling equipment is required to undertake six activities:

1. Ship loading,

2. Ship unloading,

3. Storing,

4. Reclamation,

5. Transport within the yard,

6. Transfer to other modal forms.

The dry bulk terminal will be built with sufficient quay length to give the number of berths required and of sufficient quay face strength to support the loading/discharge equipment, yard transport equipment (eg conveyor belts) and ship securing.

Due to cargo characteristics, different dry bulk materials will require different equipment. For simplicity dry bulk cargo port operations will consider cargoes having:

• low stowage factor and open storage needs e.g. iron ore and coal

• medium/high stowage factor and closed storage needs e.g. grain, and animal feedstuffs.

It is appropriate to recognise that small ports are equipped with portable systems allowing operational flexibility at low cost.

9.8.2 Ship Loaders

The process of loading a bulk cargo is basically that of pouring the cargo into the ships cargo hold in a controlled manner. Loading compared to discharge is a high speed operation with loading rates of up to 14,000 tonnes per hour occasionally being achieved for high density cargoes, such as iron ore.

The BLU Code

Prior to loading, cargo information is exchanged between ship and shore. Information exchange includes a general description of the cargo including stowage factor, angle of repose, trimming procedures, chemical properties and moisture content. The loading task is undertaken in accordance with the International Maritime Organization's **Code for the Practice of Safe Loading and Unloading of Bulk Carriers (BLU Code) 1997** which includes a Ship/Shore Safety Check-list and a standard Ship Loading Plan. The Ship Loading Plan provides details of the load sequence and ballasting operations to ensure that the ships structure is not stressed beyond stated limits during loading or discharge.

There are three principal types of ship loaders used on specialised bulk loading berths namely the fixed loader, the parallel loader and the radial loader. The basic elements of any ship loader consists of a feed elevator, a loading shute (or grab) and the force of gravity.

The **fixed loader** consists of a fixed loading shute served by a feed elevator. The bulk carrier is manoeuvred along the quayside during the loading process to ensure that the cargo is loaded in the correct sequence. It is not a common system

The **parallel loader** consists of a gantry framed structure capable of traversing along the quay length and being positioned alongside the ship's holds to be loaded in the order required by the ship's loading plan. The bulk carrier remains in position during the loading operation. Bulk cargo is moved by an elavator and conveyor system to the loading shute. A ship loader may be equipped with either telescopic vertical pipe (a cascade shute) or a spout trimming plate which permits the trimming of cargo in the hold and limits the breaking of friable cargoes.

The **radial loader**, like the parallel loader does not require the bulk carrier to be moved to enable the loading sequence to be fulfilled. As suggested by its name the radial loader is fixed at one end of its axis and can swing into position over the hold to be loaded. A telescopic loading shute enables the cargo to be positioned in the correct cargo hold and trimmed as appropriate. Radial loaders have an advantage in cost over the parallel loader as the marine supporting structure is less complex. Ease of enclosing the serving conveyors and elevators is helpful in dust reduction. However, they are limited in the length of the bulk carrier they serve and hence tend to be found in smaller ports.

Figure 9.15 – Parallel Terminal Loader

Non specialist **shore cranes**, with suitable lifting attachments, are frequently used for the handling of scrap steel, aggregates and coal from quay stockpiles.

9.8.3 Ship Unloaders

Unloading a dry bulk cargo is more difficult than loading due to the simple fact that gravity cannot be used to assist. Indeed the vertical lifts necessary have to work against the force of gravity. As a result discharge rates are slower and ship's time alongside proportionately longer. There are two principal methods of ship discharging bulk cargoes, namely grabs and continuous unloaders.

9.8.4 Grabs

Grabs for the discharge of dry bulk cargoes are attached to slewing or gantry cranes. There are a variety of grab designs but those most frequently used for dry bulk cargoes are clam shell grabs.

The **slewing crane** is usually shore located and has the ability to travel on rails along the side of the bulk carrier permitting positioning as required by the discharge plan. A clam grab attached to a slewing crane can have a capacity of fifty tonnes for iron ore. The slewing crane is often associated with a general cargo berth although it might be mobile and barge mounted. The advantages of the slewing crane over a gantry crane is that it has a lower weight, consumes less power and has relatively low maintenance costs. It also has flexibility in the forms of cargo which can be lifted.

The **gantry crane** has a lot in common with the container quayside gantry crane. A major difference lies in the end attachment, where a clam shell grab replaces the container spreader. Shore discharge is to a hopper which controls the cargo onto the land based transport. The gantry crane has a very high unloading capacity. The largest clam shell grabs have a capacity of 85 tonnes when used for the discharge of iron ore and 60 cycles per hour can be achieved. A theoretical discharge rate of 5,000 tonnes per hour per crane is possible. In practice the discharge rate is slower and will depend on many factors including the actual grab hoist speed, the skill of the operator, the shape of hold and hatch opening, the depth of hold, tidal height, travel distance from ships side to the shore hopper and stowage factor of the cargo being discharged. Many berths on a specialised bulk terminal will be equipped with two gantry cranes.

(Photo P Wright)

Figure 9.16 – Bulk Discharge Gantry Cranes – Amsterdam

Figure 9.17 – Clam Shell Bucket Grab

Mobile harbour cranes are becoming increasingly popular among port and terminal operators for bulk material handling.

9.8.5 Continuous Unloaders

An alternative to the grab is the continuous unloader. There are several basic types including the bucket wheel, screw and pneumatic. The **bucket wheel unloader** has a 'head' which cuts into the bulk cargo and transfers it to a vertical lift system for ultimate discharge. The bucket wheel has high unloading capacity typically in the order of 5,000 tonnes per hour. It is normally used in a port facility which has direct storage using a conveyor belt system for 'in port' transport. A bucket wheel unloader can handle a variety of cargoes including coal and agribulks. It has low maintenance costs. Unlike the clam grab it can reach extremes of the ship's cargo hold and hence has a high level of efficiency. The **continuous screw unloader** is a form of continuous unloader based on the principle of the screw. The screw end is the cutting head. Cargo moves along the screw as the screw is rotated. Like the bucket wheel unloader, the continuous screw unloader can reach all parts of a ship's hold. With an unloading rate of between 5,000 and 6,000 tonnes per hour it is best used for the discharge of fine powder and granulated material. The continuous screw unloader creates little dust which is a positive advantage when discharging cargoes in environmentally sensitive areas. A third type of continuous unloader is the **pneumatic unloader** which is used for the discharge of grain and powdered cargoes, such as alumina and cement. The pneumatic equipment is located on a frame which can traverse the length of the quay. Essentially a vacuum is produced in the discharge line. Atmospheric pressure acts on external cargo forcing the cargo up the discharge line. Pneumatic unloaders are dust free and have good accessibility to the cargo hold space. They are high consumers of power and cannot be used for sized cargoes.

Figure 9.18 – Bucket Wheel Unloader Head

Figure 9.19 – Bucket Wheel Unloader

9.9 DRY BULK CARGO – STORAGE

Both export and import dry bulk goods will be stored at the terminal yard. Several aspects need consideration, e.g. is storage of the commodity to be open and subject to the elements or closed and protected? How is the bulk cargo to be stacked and reclaimed from storage? What equipment is required for the transport of bulk cargo about the storage yard? How is the environment to be protected from noise and dust?

9.9.1 Open Dry Bulk Storage

Major bulks such as iron ore and coal are stored open to the elements. The shape of the storage piles will be determined by the throughput, the land area available and the terminal handling equipment. There are five recognised storage pile shapes which are used in port terminal operations and in ascending efficiency of land area used are; the conical pile, the radial pile, single wind row pile, double wind row pile and block pile. Conical and radial pile storages are used in port operations where throughput is small and port equipment is mainly of a portable type. Single wind row, double wind row and block pile are used on major bulk import terminals where storage needs are both transitory and strategic.

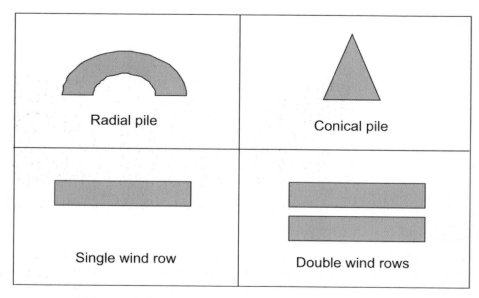

Figure 9.20 – Bulk Storage Pile Configurations

9.9.2   Stacker

The type of equipment used to create the pile formations stated above differs. There are three basic equipment types used, namely the conical conveyor, the stacker and the gantry.

The **conical stacker and radial stacker** comprise of an elevator which allows the bulk commodity to be lifted to a determined height and poured from that height to form a conical pile. The precise shape of the pile will be determined by the angle of repose of the commodity. The maximum height of the cone is determined by the height of the lip of the chute. The **radial stacker** is an elevator similar to the above which can be rotated horizontally through 180°. By being rotated the cone is distributed in a semi-circular manner. The height of the radial pile is determined by the height of the lip of the shute, the radius by the length of the radial conveyor arm and the shape by the angle of repose of the commodity. The single stacker is used to create a single wind row pile. The **single stacker** consists of a frame structure which traverses horizontal rails. It is fed by a belt conveyor which runs between the rails. A boom supporting the stacking belt conveyor is mounted at right angles to the feed conveyor and distributes the commodity to the pile. The vertical height of the boom can be adjusted to maximise the yard area used for storage. The frame structure incorporates a driver's cab which is used to control the movement of the single stacker. A **double stacker** is used to create a double wind row. The construction of a double stacker is similar to the single stacker but in addition the double stacker has two conveyor booms feeding from the central conveyor. The conveyor arms are positioned at 180° to each other and are able to create two adjacent and parallel piles. The double stacker is used in large storage areas. The block pile which provides the most land efficient method of storage will use a **gantry crane**. The width of the block pile is determined by the gantry span.

Figure 9.21 – A Stacker Showing Double Wind Row Open Storage

9.9.3 Reclaimer

There will be a need to reclaim a stored bulk commodity from a pile. This task will be undertaken by different means. At a basic level a front-end **dumper truck** or shovel loader can be used. At the largest dry bulk terminals where storage in wind and double wind piles is used specialised reclaimers will be used. A **reclaimer** consists of a bucket wheel located at the end of a boom. The bucket wheel cuts into the stored cargo through a boom conveyor belt and a hopper directs it onto the yard conveyor belt system. It is then moved to where it is needed e.g. the ship, barge, loader or rail head.

Figure 9.22 – Dry Bulk Yard Reclaimer

The reclaimer like the stacker is a substantive piece of equipment. It is rail mounted to allow transfer within the storage yard. Certain equipment design may provide inter-changeability of the roles of stacking and reclamation by the same piece of equipment.

Other dry bulk terminal equipment includes the hopper and the conveyor belt. The hopper is used in conjunction with a non continuous unloader e.g. clam shell grab to direct and control the flow of the bulk commodity either onto the yard conveyor belt system or into rail trucks.

(Photo: P Wright)

Figure 9.23 – Bulk Yard Hoppers Spanning a Yard Conveyor System

The **conveyor belt** provides an economic means of transport within the terminal yard allowing large quantities of cargo to be moved continuously both into and away from storage piles. A conveyor system is a complex structure comprising of a rubber belt shaped and supported by idlers. A pulley system transmits power to the belt and trippers used to change directional flow of the bulk. Conveyor belts commonly used in bulk terminal yards have a capacity to move between 7,000 and 8,000 tonnes of commodity per hour, depending on material density.

9.9.4   Closed Dry Bulk Storage

Cargoes which are sensitive to damp are stored in closed dry bulk warehouses or silos. There are many designs from the single storey warehouse to the bulk silo. Storage requirements will be specific to a particular cargo. Mixed dry bulk cargo storage will demand a more flexible approach. Critical to storage is the need for segregation and cleanliness. Large scale bulk warehouse storage uses overhead conveyors to feed individual bins within the warehouse. Bulk grain is typically stored in concrete silos using pneumatic to move the cargo from the ship unloaders to the silos. Discharge of the silo to road or rail transport is controlled by a horizontal gate. Port storage of grain is undertaken on a massive scale. A recently completed grain terminal complex in Dalian, China provides storage for more than 400,000 tonnes in 128 separate silos.

9.9.5   Dust and Noise Reduction

There are two principle environmental issues associated with dry bulk cargoes, namely noise during loading/discharging and dust at all stages of the operation including storage. Dust is a particular problem for cargoes which are stored on open terminals. eg. iron ore and coal. Wind causes dust distribution which can be a considerable nuisance to adjacent properties and terminals. Computer controlled dampening systems, which allow water to be sprayed onto the storage piles are used to minimise these issues.

Figure 9.24 – Covered Conveyors Limit the Dust Nuisance

For transport from storage to ships side the dust nuisance can be reduced by the use of covered conveyor belts. Dust control at the point of loading (normally associated with cargoes of a powdery nature) is maintained by a dust suppressor. This is a twin walled loading spout, the duct between the two walls conveys the dust laden air from the loads surface and a flexible skirt at the spout end which seals the loading operation.

9.10   LIQUID BULK CARGO TERMINALS

9.10.1   Terminal Equipment

The port terminal is where the loading, discharge and storage of liquid bulk cargoes takes place. Liquid bulk cargo can be classified as **primary** products, such as mineral, vegetable and animal oils and **processed** products, such as oil products, chemicals, wines and rubber (latex) In addition liquefied gases are handled and stored in port areas. Terminal equipment is required to undertake various activities at the interface including:

- ship loading,

- ship unloading,

- transport within the terminal,

- storing,

- transfer to other modes of transport.

The wet bulk terminal, consists of a single jetty berth or a number of jetty berths for tankers to lay alongside, tank storage facilities, pipelines, control systems and emergency equipment. There are four main types of jetty berths, namely the shore linked "T" Jetty, the water linked jetty, the Single Point Mooring (SPM) and lineal quayage. Jetty berths are normally allocated for a single purpose, but may be grouped within a terminal structure to provide facilities required by different users e.g. deep sea tankers, coastal tankers and river craft.

Figure 9.25 – The Shore Linked 'T' Jetty Berth

9.10.2   The Jetty Berth

Jetty berths are designed for a tanker to lay alongside. The normal jetty berth is a pylon structure which supports a platform on which is placed the loading or discharge arms (known as "chicksans"), fire monitors and a control room. The midships body of the tanker will lie on the berth. Securing lines are made fast to strategically located dolphins positioned in line with the berth and connected to the berth by walkways. The jetty berth will have sufficient strength to absorb the kinetic force of the tanker "landing" on it, The tanker's speed of approach on to the berth may be controlled by using information from a berthing system. A fendering system will absorb the final energy on "landing" and protect both berth and ship from damage due to ship surge and ranging whilst alongside. The jetty berth is usually located some distance from the shore to ensure sufficient water for the loaded tanker. The jetty berth is usually connected to the shore by a trestle structure which accommodates pipelines and roadway access. In water linked jetties, the berth and dolphins will not be connected to the shore. In such case the berth will be accessed by water transport and the pipelines will be submerged. Larger terminals may have "stand-by" emergency tugs on station available to give support in case of oil spillage, fire or explosion.

9.10.3   Ship Loading/Unloading Equipment

Cargo is loaded to, and unloaded from the tanker by connecting the terminal pipelines to the ship's manifold using either a "chicksan" or a flexible hose.

Figure 9.26 – Chicksans and Manifold Ship/Shore Connection

The chicksan is a complex piece of equipment which connects the shore pipeline to the ships manifold, the capacity of which can be in the order of 6,000 tonnes per hour. The chicksan has a counterweight balance to minimise the connecting stress at the ships manifold and to accommodate the tanker's raning movement on the jetty berth due to tidal height change, wind and loading condition. An operational 'ranging' envelope is defined for a chicksan. If operation takes place outside the envelope there is a risk of failure and spillage. Instant warning and remote failsafe devices, including safety shut-off and emergency release are incorporated into the design. Flexible pipelines are sometimes used, normally between ship and barge.

9.10.4   Terminal Pipeline Systems

At multi commodity berths (e.g. liquid chemicals), it is critical that risk of contamination between cargo types is eliminated. This is achieved using a designated pipeline system for each cargo type, an expensive option. Ensuring the highest standard of cleanliness of terminal pipelines is critical. Pipeline cleansing is undertaken by fresh water purging and the use of a 'pig' (a rubber or sponge plug). The 'pig' is inserted and forced through the pipeline by pressurised inert gas.

Loading of a tanker is normally by gravity flow from the shore storage tanks whilst discharge is undertaken using pumps carried by the tanker. The shore terminal will be equipped with **pumps** for the purposes of moving cargoes within the terminal.

No liquid bulk terminal can be without means of **storage**. Port storage uses cylindrical tanks the capacity of which can vary from 60 tonnes to 150,000 tonnes. Over time a bulk liquid cargo will evaporate to the atmosphere. Storage tanks are designed to minimise evaporation. There are two principal types of storage tank, namely the fixed roof tank and the floating roof tank.

9.10.5   The Fixed Roof Tank

This tank is the simplest and cheapest to produce. The fixed roof tank consists of cylindrical steel or concrete walls with a roof. It is sited on a concrete floor separated from its surrounds by an impervious membrane. When liquid is held in a tank it will rarely occupy all the space available. Stored liquid gives off vapour which causes pressure on the tank. The tank is built to withstand a certain pressure. If that pressure is exceeded or conversely is vacuum created in the tank, there is risk of explosion or implosion. A fixed roof storage tank will be fitted with Pressure Vacuum (P/V) valve on the roof to ensure that calculated pressure and vacuum levels are not exceeded. Change in pressure is also caused during loading and discharging and by the daily change of temperature. The measurement of the tank ullage, from which the amount of cargo held in the tank can be calculated is established using a float gauge or tank radar system mounted on the tank roof. Also on the roof will be a manhole which provides entry to the tank. A manhole is also provided at ground level for entry into an empty tank as is a nozzle for drainage of excess decanted water A shore storage tank is bottom loaded.

(Photo: P Wright)

Figure 9.27 – Floating Roof 'Crude Oil' Tanks Each With a Capacity of 150,000 Tonnes

9.10.6   The Floating Roof Tank

A floating roof tank consists of a cylindrical steel or concrete wall cylinder. The roof floats on the stored liquid with an airtight seal established between the cylindrical walls and the roof assembly. The space between the liquid surface and the underside of the roof is minimal therefore restricting vapour loss through evaporation. The floating roof automatically compensates for variations in vapour pressure due to loading, discharging and daily change in temperature. As a result a PV valve is not required and losses through evaporation are minimised. There are different designs of floating roof, including the steel pan, the aluminium pontoon and buoyancy rim roof. Gauging is undertaken from a fixed external point on the cylinder wall. A drainage system to disperse accumulated rain from the central main drain on the floating roof is incorporated into the design. Access to the roof is provided by a hinged walkway. Some storage tank designs incorporate a floating roof within a fixed roof structure.

Some liquids require to be maintained at a temperature above or below ambient temperature. In the case of **heated tanks**, steam heating coils are fitted at the base of the tank. Steam is produced by a boiler separate to the tank. It passes through the heating coils to maintain above ambient temperature of the liquid. Temperature sensors within the tank provide data to allow control of the heat required. A heated tank is usually of a fixed roof type and will be heavily insulated to minimise heat loss or gain.

Storage of **below ambient temperature** liquid cargoes is limited and normally associated with liquefied gases. Tanks required for storage will have heavy ground, wall and roof insulation. Refrigeration equipment will be required to maintain the low temperatures required.

9.10.7 Terminal Safety

> **Terminal Safety**
>
> Terminal operations concerning petroleum, chemicals and liquefied gases present dangers to property and persons. Rules and regulations which have been established help minimise risk. Well trained port operatives and properly maintained equipment also help reduce danger. The topic of safety is large and is covered in publications including the **International Safety Guide for Oil Tankers and Terminals 2006 (ISGOTT Manual)** and the **International Safety Guide for Liquefied Gas Tankers and Terminals**

Protection of the **environment** is a concern to the terminal operator. Issues concern the failure and leakage of the tank structure, run-off and emissions. To minimise the impact of **leakage** from a storage tank, the tank or a number of tanks will be placed within a bund. The volume of space within the bund having sufficient capacity to retain the total capacity of the storage tank or tanks Rain water **run-off** on a terminal will spread any minor oil spillage into the surrounding area. A liquid bulk terminal will be equipped with an enclosed drainage system. in which run-off is collected and decanted before free water is released. Disposal of the oil or chemical residue can then be effectively undertaken. At a modal transfer point and where purging of tank gases takes place there is risk of **emission** to the atmosphere. It is becoming an industry standard to provide a closed system, so that vapour emitted can be collected and reduced to a liquid. Such a system is known as vapour recovery.

The liquid bulk terminal will connect storage to **other transport modes** namely, pipeline, road, rail or barge. The need for flexibility will depend on the commodity range. At liquid chemical and product terminals the integrated nature is such that all transport modes are used, whereas the transport method used from a crude oil terminal will normally be by pipeline.

(Photo: Vopak)

(Photo: P Wright)

Figure 9.28 – Inland Waterway Barge Used for Transport of Liquid Bulk Cargo

Figure 9.29 – Road Tankers Used for Transport of Liquid Bulk Cargo

It may be appropriate to carry certain dry cargoes in **slurry (liquefied)** form which can produce certain economic advantages to the shipper and receiver. Port equipment usually consists of slurry storage tanks and loading equipment.

9.11 FUTURE CHALLENGES IN SHIP AND CARGO HANDLING

The past four decades have seen dramatic changes in the ports industry. In general it has changed from being a manpower intensive industry based on cheap labour costs using limited technology to being highly capital intensive. Advanced technology is embraced to ensure that its role in the supply chain is managed at the highest level of efficiency. Ports have adapted their facilities with the needs of their customers in mind. Specialist ship designs have forced the development of specialised terminal facilities. Without the changes which have occurred, it is inconceivable that the growth in world trade would have progressed as it has done.

Looking to the future is difficult. Almost a quarter of a century ago MacGreggor Publications published a book **"Ships and Shipping of Tomorrow"**. Whilst many of the innovations suggested have already been achieved, there are still some concepts which could be considered to enhance future port efficiency.

With respect to **unitised cargoes** it is unlikely that we will see a fundamental change in the use of the ISO standard container. However, limited land space will drive the need for automation and more intensive use of port terminals. Economic factors will limit the maximum size of the present design of a cellular container ship. The size of the post-panamax cellular container ship is expected to grow. The 11,000 TEU ship is already present and designs for a 13,500 TEU Malaccamax ship are already on the drawing board. The larger ships will be limited in the number of ports which will be able to accommodate them. Continuous horizontal flows of containers between ship and shore, the multiple lifting of individual containers, or high intensity Lift-On Lift-Off systems might be used to increase terminal throughput. A reduced number of hub ports requiring the development of more sophisticated terminals for feeder operation is likely. Niche markets will make use of innovative hull forms in the unitised and RO-RO sector of the short sea and feeder service routes. The rapid flow of cargo information on secure networks will be critical.

In the **dry bulk sector** new innovations regarding discharge of certain bulk cargoes could be used e.g. the specialist discharge of ore into a bulk discharge dock. In the **liquid bulk sector**, particularly concerning the movement of crude oil, environmental interests will dominate. The double hull has yet to prove its long term viability. Future tanker designs will evolve and may be required to have greater sub-division of cargo spaces, be built to higher standards, use inert gas within the double hull void spaces and be required to have a twin main propulsion system. New methods of transporting gas under pressure (rather than reduced temperature) are presently being evaluated. In the **passenger** sector the cruise market is set to develop further, with new innovations in size, luxury and novelty being driving factors. More ports will be required to service the cruise ship sector.

The challenges for **port management** will continue as world trade continues to grow. Pressure will be exerted on available waterfront sites, competition between ports sharing the same hinterland increased, pressures on the physical environment will be recognised and security against terrorist threat is needed.

9.12 SELF-ASSESSMENT AND TEST QUESTIONS

Attempt the following and check your answers from the text.

1. Expand the following abbreviations (i) RMG (ii) RTG and (iii) AGV.

2. List the basic requirements to be considered by Port Management when evaluating the type of container yard system to use.

3. Describe and explain why in particular shipping sectors the pallet may provide the optimum system for cargo unitisation. Give examples.

4. Define the phrases "stowage factor" "moisture content" and "angle of repose". Describe their significance with respect to the storage of dry bulk cargoes in port.

5. State the advantages and disadvantages of the THREE common type of ship loaders used at port bulk terminals.

6. Briefly explain the contents and purposes of the BLU Code.

7. List the activities undertaken at a marine bulk liquid terminal.

8. What is a 'chicksan' and what parameters have to be considered in its design?

9. The measurement quantities of a liquid bulk cargo transferred between ship and shore are rarely the same. Explain.

10. *"For the future health of the port, the port manager needs to maintain a continuing awareness of development in ships, technology and the world economy".*

    Discuss this statement with reference to a port with which you are familiar or have an interest.

    The above narrative has described the systems and equipment used by ports for the transfer and storage of bulk liquid, bulk dry and unitised cargoes. The author acknowledges that the descriptions are limited and that the operation of specific terminals associated with the handling of forest products, automobiles, steel and perishable have not been covered.

By completing the Chapter the student will have gained an awareness and appreciation of the extent of operational activities in which a port is involved.

Having completed Chapter Nine attempt ONE of the following and submit the answer to your Tutor.

1. Describe and discuss the handling equipment appropriate for use on a multi-purpose terminal and that required by a high density container terminal.

2. For either a Dry Bulk Terminal or a Liquid Bulk Terminal list the handling equipment required and explain the operational problems which may be encountered.

PORT OWNERSHIP

10.1   INTRODUCTION

Chapter Ten reviews the issue of Port Ownership and considers the value of port privatisation and deregulation

10.2   TYPES OF OWNERSHIP

Ports can be owned privately, publicly or as a mixture of the two. In 1999 the International Association of Ports and Harbours surveyed its members (which include most of the world's major ports and many medium sized ones) and found that over 90% were public organisations. This is in accordance with the accepted wisdom that a port, being a natural monopoly, should be in public ownership and operated for the benefit of the public as a whole. Infrastructure is built and maintained as a public good with free public access. In addition, ports are strategic assets which need to be under national control.

10.2.1   Public Ownership

Ports can be considered under three broad types:

1.   Government owned ports

2.   Autonomous (Trust) Ports

3.   Municipal Ports

Government Owned ports are ports in which the national government has a direct interest. There are several different models of government ownership which includes:

- **Direct government control:** Direct control by government allows for the national planning of ports. Whilst it should result in the best use of limited national resources and avoidance of duplication (because of political sensitivities) direct government control can result in over manning, under investment and general inefficiency.

- **Government owned corporation:** Whilst still owned by the national government, the Corporation undertakes to run the port as a commercial entity. A hands-off model which allows the port managers a greater flexibility, the government owning the port as a corporation may be the prelude to a partial or complete privatisation of the port.

- **Majority government shareholding:** A third model of government ownership is when the government maintains a majority shareholding (or 'golden share') in a private company.

Autonomous (Trust) Ports. In the United Kingdom a public trust can be established by an Act of Parliament. A trust port is an organisation run by a Board elected or appointed from local stakeholders. London and Liverpool used to be trust ports, but lacking the freedom to raise capital needed for modern port investment they moved into the private sector. In the United Kingdom only smaller ports remain as trust ports. UK trust ports were privatised between 1991 and 1997. In France the government granted autonomous status to six major ports in 1966. Whilst state-owned they control their own finances.

Municipal Ports Rotterdam, Hamburg and Kobe are owned by the municipality (city) of which they are a part. Municipal ownership allows close co-operation between the port and city but can hamper national planning because the port authority will respond to local political priorities. A municipal port will generate its income from sea and inland port dues, quay dues rental and leasehold revenues from sites within the port area. The internal management organisation of a municipal port is comprehensive and will cover commercial development, strategic planning and research and shipping.

10.2.2 Private Ownership

This type of port is considered under three broad types;

1.   Public Limited Company,

2.   Subsidiary of a Parent Company,

3.   Long Term Lease.

A **Public Limited Company** will own all the land and infrastructure including the quays. The Felixstowe Dock and Railway Company was privately owned from the start. It is now part of the Hutchison Whampoa Group.

A **Subsidiary of a Parent Company.** Commodity ports are often owned by the mining company that ships its cargoes through them. Such ports can be seen as a cost centre to the parent firm.

A **Long Term Lease** from the state or municipality. In 1991 the port of Bristol was leased by the City of Bristol to a private firm, the Bristol Port Company. The lease is for 150 years.

10.3   THE MOVEMENT TO DEREGULATE PORTS

In Chapter One the effects of globalisation on ports were explained and can be summarised as:

- an increase in the volume of world trade,

- changes in the pattern of world trade as manufacturing moves East,

- demand for fast, reliable delivery of goods on a just-in-time basis, cutting the cost of stocks held in transit and in buffer warehouses,

- cost cutting at every point of the supply chain, leading to containerisation, increase of ship size, quicker throughput at ports, and more efficient communication,

- an increase in competition between ports, and between the different modes of transport – sea, land and air,

- private terminal operators are investing in ports on a global basis resulting in standard, high quality, low-cost services.

To meet the challenge of globalisation, ports have to increase both capacity and efficiency while reducing costs. Traditionally, ports were not only publicly owned but also politically controlled and regulated. This replaces the possibility of market failure (because the port is a monopoly and not subject to competitive disciplines) with state failure: inefficient ports, choking trade and development. There are two possible remedies, deregulation or privatisation.

Deregulation is the reduction of the role of government in an enterprise, with market forces replacing government regulation as the guarantor of acceptable industry performance. This section deals with the trend towards deregulation of ports.

Labour reform in docks is intimately tied up with problems of government control and efficiency. Under public control, the stated objectives of port management are often concerned with developing the regional economy and maintaining employment.

In the nineteenth century dock work was casual with no security or continuity of employment. As labour became more organised, dock workers' unions were able to organise strikes and create unrest. Dock strikes particularly undertaken on a national basis can be very damaging to a country dependent on trade. Militant dock unions in the industrial nations of the world were able to gain tight control over wages, working practices and employment levels. In the UK, the National Dock Labour Scheme made it impossible to shed excess labour without very large compensation payments being made. The shipping revolution of the 1960s had its impact on the demand for port labour. In particular the development of containerisation, the growth of ship size and the increasing role of technology in cargo handling systems and information transfer saw a dramatic decrease in the demand for dock labour. Technical investment has changed the status of the port employee and provided a more secure working environment.

The process of labour reform is an essential part of the drive towards low-cost, efficient ports. It is politically difficult where the ports are under the direct control of local or central government. Disengaging ports from direct control is often seen as a necessary prelude to labour reform.

Modern ports require very high levels of investment if they are to remain competitive. Investment in the basic infrastructure of capital dredging (the initial deepening of a channel), breakwaters, road and rail access, are clearly public works for the public good. This leaves the provision of cranes, warehouses, computer systems, stevedoring services, security services and port navigation services (all traditionally provided by the state at a cost to the taxpayer) which could be provided by the private sector if the legal status of the port allowed it. However, port legislation dating from the middle of the twentieth century or earlier was frequently restrictive with a control structure that gave little or no leeway for the ports to manage their own financial affairs. New laws were needed to loosen the restrictions on ports and allow them the freedom to raise and invest money, dispose of surplus assets and take partners from the private sector who could bring in trade if they were a shipping company or had management expertise and money.

Moving any business from the public to the private sector is claimed to increase efficiency. Deep inefficiencies in state run ports in developing countries contrast badly with the performance of privately operated terminals in the developed world. In the state sector, port managers are hired on contracts which offer job security, but without performance incentives. Port management may fall into a cosy consensus with the workforce so that no-one has to work too hard to keep their jobs. In the private sector, management have to go to the capital markets to finance investment, where they compete for funds with other businesses. If funding cannot be self-financed they have to be able to convince the financial institutions that they can run the business profitably. In addition, market discipline is enforced by shareholders who will sell up if the company is unprofitable. The share price will fall and the company will be in danger of being taken over and the managers sacked.

There have been problems in introducing private management at ports in some countries such as Thailand and India because central port administrations and labour unions have fought against the loss of their privileges.

Over the last twenty years as a result of globalisation and its demands for efficient, low-cost and capital intensive ports, there has been a trend towards deregulation. Ports need the freedom to reform labour, raise capital and manage themselves in response to commercial rather than political pressures. The monopoly argument has been lost with the growth of port hinterlands and competition from other modes. Few ports are now in a monopoly position. In addition the abuse of a public monopoly (e.g. by port labour) has proved as bad as the abuse of private monopoly. Many states have retained ownership of port land, but there is an accelerating trend towards a loosening of government control and mixed public/private ownership. Offering 'concessions' to specialist port operating companies to run a port terminal, owned by a government (usually for a fixed period of time) is a further way in which deregulation can be achieved.

10.3.1   Privatisation of Ports

Privatisation is the actual sale of an asset, or the right to provide a service to the private sector. Full privatisation can take place in three ways:

- **Stock Market Flotation**

    This clearly specifies that the objective of the firm is to make profits, it introduces the threat of bankruptcy and replaces political involvement with financial markets monitoring the commercial outcomes.

- **Management/Employee Buy-Out**

    Debt and quasi-debt instruments are used to enable management and their financial backers to purchase a controlling equity in the company. The management have an incentive to make profits, the financiers provide external oversight and employees are involved in monitoring and possibly raising efficiency.

- **Third Party or Trade Sale**

    The port may not be initially profitable, or there may be economies of scale or gains from vertical integration.

During the 1980s the political agenda in the United Kingdom was to disengage the state from business as much as possible. This led to a wave of privatisations including the privatisation of ports. Privatisation led to the ports owned by the government and operated by the British Transport Docks Board (BTDB) being reconstituted and registered under the Companies Act as Associated British Ports. In 1983 Associated British Ports (ABP) was floated on the London Stock Exchange. Other ports owned by the government, (notably the railway ports) were sold to private buyers including the American shipping line Sea Containers Ltd.

The largest Trust ports of the United Kingdom were privatised after 1991 in response to pressure from the ports themselves. The ports petitioned the government to become private in order for them to push through reforms, and improve their ability to raise money for development purposes.

Privatisation of Ports: UK CASE STUDIES

Case Study 1: The ABP Sale

After World War II the Labour government nationalised public utilities, heavy industries, such as coal and steel and transport enterprises including ports. The British Transport Docks Board (BTDB) was established as a direct agency of the government responsible for managing nineteen ports. In one of the earliest privatisations of the 1979 elected Conservative government under the Transport Act of 1981 BTDB was incorporated as Associated British Ports (ABP). In 1983 52% of the company was offered for sale in a public share issue. Shares were oversubscribed by 34 times, indicating that the price had been set too low. The sale realised £22 million. The remaining shares were sold in April 1984 for £52 million. ABP has subsequently become the leading UK ports company with a turnover in 2004 of £350 Million. In 2006 ABP was subject to takeover bids by Dubai Ports World and Goldman Sachs who valued the company at about $2.8 Billion.

Case Study 2: The Sealink Ports

*It was quite common for railway companies to own businesses connected with transport such as ports, ferry companies and hotels. When the separate railway companies were nationalised the ports they owned became part of **British Rail**. Although British Rail was not privatised until 1993, government policy encouraged the sale of its non-rail businesses during the 1980s. British Rail ports were transferred to Sealink Harbours Ltd. After £8 million of debt had been wiped out from Sealink Harbours Ltd, the ports had been independently valued at between £110 and £120 million. They were put up for auction and twelve bidders competed for the company. The highest* *bidder was Sea Containers who offered and paid £60 Million. Three of the ports were later taken over by the Swedish ferry operator Stena.*

Case Study 3: Privatising the Municipal Ports

In 1989 new legislation required local authorities that owned municipal ports to set up a separate operating company. The ports had to be run on commercial lines without subsidy. Although most of these ports remain under local authority ownership, loss making ports had to be disposed of. In 1991, Bristol leased its loss-making docks at Royal Portbury and Avonmouth to a private company on a 150 year lease. The new Bristol Port Company increased revenue by 60% in three years and made £150 million on it's investment. The Bristol Port Company is innovative and making use of the location and extensive transport links and is presently planning a new deep water container terminal capable of handling ships of up to 12,500 TEU.

Case Study 4: Medway. A Trust Port which became a Private Port

The 1991 Ports Privatisation Act paved the way for the largest Trust Ports to be privatised. Each Trust Board organised the privatisation process for their own port. The Trustees had to set themselves up as an incorporated company and then sell the company through a bidding process. Half the money raised went to the government, and half went to the port. The successful bidder was not necessarily the highest bidder as the Port Privatisation Act stated 'that priority would be given to Management/Employee Buy Outs'. The Trust could value the port, sell it to themselves and then receive half the purchase price. The port of Medway was sold to a Management/Employee Buy Out, the only bidder for £28.7 million. It was later sold on to the Mersey Dock and Harbour Company for £104 million.

10.3.2 The Sale of State Ports to the Private Sector

The sale of national assets to the private sector has not been without its critics. It is useful to consider the reasons for and against such sales. The arguments put forward are listed below:

Arguments FOR the Sale of State Owned Ports:

1. Expansion of ports is difficult as state owned facilities cannot raise money on the money markets,

2. Private management is more efficient,

3. Trust ports are unable to diversify or utilise idle land and resources,

4. Competition is increased leading to greater productivity,

5. Management/Employee Buy Outs give employees a stake in their own business,

6. Money is raised to fund other public activities,

7. Political interference is eliminated.

Arguments AGAINST the Sale of State owned Ports:

1. Profits should be re-invested in the ports, not handed out to shareholders,

2. State owned and Trust ports have access to cheap capital from local authorities and government,

3. The dock labour reforms which took place in the United Kingdom in 1988 was the most important factor in improving port efficiency. Cock labour reform is independent of privatisation,

4. Port diversification could be permitted by a small change in the law without the need for full port privatisation,

5. Valuation of ports is difficult particularly if it includes the seaward port approaches Prices paid for State owned ports in the United Kingdom were little more than guesswork and generally too low,

6. Income received by the State for a port sale is too small to make the exercise worthwhile.

7. Ports have an environmental and public good role to play which is more appropriate for the public sector,

8. Governments have no right to sell ports which belong to their local community

10.3.3 Deregulation with Partial Privatisation

The most common response to the pressures of globalisation is to deregulate with partial privatisation. The basic model allows a port to maintain ownership of the port but its commercial operation is released from political control. The commercial operation will be exposed to market forces.

Partial privatisation of a port may use one or more of the following methods:

1. Concessions,

2. Joint Ventures,

3. Commercialisation,

4. Corporatisation,

5. Build-Operate-Transfer,

6. Management Contracts.

10.3.4 Concessions

A concession is *'a contractual arrangement in which government retains the ultimate ownership of assets and transfers some or all of the commercial risk of operating the asset to a private concessionaire'.* The contract will have defined terms and agreement will exist to describe the objectives and risk allocation of the concession.

Risk allocation is the core of a concession agreement and concerns commercial risk, country risk and exchange rate risks,

Commercial risk is caused by uncertainty over future traffic levels. It is lower in a concession where existing facilities are taken over. The construction of a new terminal poses a higher level of uncertainty, but in this case concessionaires often include a shipping line which can guarantee to bring in trade from its own ships.

Country risk arises from uncertainty about the security situation of a country (as with Aden in Yemen) or uncertainty about the commitment of a government to a project. Where a government has a history of demanding changes in the face of public pressure, financing will be harder to obtain.

Exchange rate risk is rarely a problem with ports because tariffs are normally paid in dollars. However, the foreign concessionaire will demand guarantees that it can repatriate profits.

Exclusive rights are an important issue in a concession. Where there are several terminals in a port, competition will exist between the terminal operators. It is usually a condition that the concessionaire for a new terminal does not already operate in the port. There will then be no problem about giving the operator exclusive rights for their line to use their own terminal. In other cases it is intended for a terminal to be a common user facility, and safeguards for this must be carefully written in to the contract.

The *length of the concession* varies with the type. If the concessionaire is simply operating an existing facility it will normally be between 5 and 15 years in length. If capital investments are required as in a Repair-Operate-Transfer or Build-Operate-Transfer arrangement the company operating the concession must be able to recoup its investment. The length of the concession may be between 30 and 50 years. The shorter the concession, the more competitive pressure there will be on the firm. Governments can make a concession less than the economic life of an investment if they guarantee to buy-out assets at the end of the concession period. That will also encourage good maintenance to keep up the value. Long concessions run the risk of regulatory capture in which the private operator and the regulators will develop a relationship that interferes with proper regulation.

Ending a concession can be done in several ways but costs are involved. A premature ending of a concession will need to be undertaken with particular care. Costs will be involved in the government calling for new bids and there will be risks in losing trained and experienced staff. If performance by the concessionaire has been acceptable, automatic renewal of the concession is likely to be granted. Competitive pressure can be maintained simply by the process of re-negotiating the contract If a new bidding process is put in place the old concessionaire may be bought out, or may receive the value of their own bid from the successful bidder with the balance of the bid going to the government.

Problems with concessions usually arise through lack of preparation or over-optimistic traffic forecasts. Restructuring by incorporation, labour reform and the creation of an adequate regulatory system needs to be completed in advance of the tendering process. A successful concession is sustainable and avoids legal challenges. Post-award disputes can cause changes in the agreement, changes in the composition of a consortium, costly delays, and in the worst case may result in termination of the agreement. If this occurs the government will be forced to pick up the pieces.

10.3.5 Joint Ventures

A joint venture is an arrangement between the port authority and a port operating company to be jointly involved in the operation of the port. China and Vietnam favour joint ventures as a vehicle for building and operating new terminals. For example Shanghai Port Authority and Hutchison Whampoa formed a joint venture between subsidiaries to own and operate all of Shanghai's container port facilities. The joint venture is a 50-50 agreement, with preferential development rights for new deep-water terminals. During the first year of operation the joint venture handled 25% more containers and raised productivity by 30% more than in the previous year.

Joint ventures have been negotiated at Shekou, the port of Chiwan, Hainan Island, Daxie Island, the port of Tianjin and Yangtze River ports among others. The main partners are Dubai Ports, major shipping lines, investors from Hong Kong, Hutchison Whampoa and International Container Terminal Services Inc. of the Philippines. Joint ventures can include the provision of management expertise in such matters as dredging and other port-related services, environmental management and safety. The Port of Brisbane has entered into one such agreement with the Government of Vietnam.

10.3.6 Commercialisation

The government through a port authority continues to own facilities, but the port authority becomes more commercial in its outlook. Management and accounting principles as used in the private sector are applied.

10.3.7 Corporatisation

The first step to a full or part private sale of the port. It may also be used where there is intention to keep a port under State ownership but arrange concessions for terminal operation. Regulatory functions may be split-off from the port company to a new state body.

10.3.8   Build-Operate-Transfer

Build-Operate-Transfer (BOT) or Build-Own-Operate-Transfer (BOOT) leases are a relatively new approach to direct private sector investment in large scale port development projects. A 50 year Build- Operate-Transfer Lease has been agreed by the Port of Le Havre for its Port 2000 Project involving the development of a new container terminal. Another of this type of ownership arrangement is the Repair-Own-Transfer (ROT) lease which is used where facilities have fallen into disrepair, as at the port of Maputo.

10.3.9   Management Contract

The use of a management contract creates a degree of partial privatisation by an outside operator providing management expertise to the port.

10.3.10   Global Port Container Terminal Operators

The growth of global port container operators is a recent development. Active global companies include Dubai Ports World, Port of Singapore Corporation, (PSA), Hutchinson Port and APM (Maersk) Terminals. Drewry Consultants have estimated that by 2008 these four companies will control about thirty per cent of the world's container port capacity.

10.4   CONCLUSION

In conclusion not all state owned port enterprises are inefficient. The port of Singapore was one of the most efficient and successful ports of the world while it was still under direct state control. There are many other examples of high-performing public enterprises in ports. Research has shown that, although private ports tend to be more successful than state-run service ports, ownership is less important than organisation.

Privatisation can reduce the debt burden of developing countries by raising capital and eliminating the need for subsidies. Costs are involved in privatisation as a stock exchange flotation will involve agency costs and the costs of discounting the new share prices at the time of flotation. In a developed economy, such as the United Kingdom there can be difficulties in the valuation of port assets. This will be more acute in developing countries. Partial privatisations takes time and expertise to plan. A new regulatory role for the state will be required. When a partial privatisation fails, the state has to pick up the pieces. The process of privatisation provides an opportunity for corruption.

Two factors in today's world are putting pressure to change the form of port ownership. The first is *globalisation* which demands ports increase capacity and to utilise their capacity in ways that are more efficient. The second factor is that of *perception*. Where **once a port was perceived as a strategic asset, owned and operated by the state for the public good, a port is now seen as a commercial enterprise needing to be managed as a business**. The result is a shift to deregulate and privatise. The first step is always to turn the port into a corporation. After that a range of instruments are available to the government and port authority to assist the move towards privatisation. The extent of privatisation within a port will depend on the culture of the port and the political will of the government.

10.5   SELF-ASSESSMENT AND TEST QUESTIONS

Attempt the following and check your answers from the text.

1.   What is meant by the 'deregulation' of ports?

2.   Name three ports in each of the following categories (i) state-owned port (ii) private port (iii) partially privatised.

3.   What do the following stand for: MEBO, BOOT and ROT?

4.   Who owns a trust port?

Having completed Chapter Ten, attempt the following and submit your answer to your Tutor.

1. You have been employed as a consultant to a developing country to advise on the privatisation of their largest and loss making port. The choice is between a stock market flotation of the whole port or the leases as a concession.

2. Write a <u>report</u> setting out the advantages and disadvantages of each method with your recommendation.

THE INSTITUTE OF CHARTERED SHIPBROKERS

MOCK EXAMINATION

Do not turn to the next page until you have followed the suggestions set out below.

Overleaf is a sample examination paper. In your own interest do not look at it yet but instead do the same revision of the course as you would do for any examination.

On completing your revision put away your notes, have pen and paper ready and set aside three hours when you will not be interrupted. In other words create as near as possible examination room conditions.

It is recommended that you hand write this mock examination. You will have to write the actual examination and many students find that it is difficult to write legibly for three hours without practice. If your writing is illegible you will lose marks. Examiners cannot mark what they cannot read.

Carry out the instructions on the question paper and send your answers to your tutor for marking. (Note your start and finish times on the front of your answer paper).

THE PURPOSE AND SCOPE OF THIS BOOK AND COURSE GUIDE

AIM

1) To ensure a thorough knowledge and understanding of Port and Terminal Management.

2) To develop relevant communication skills.

PORTS AND THEIR FUNCTIONS

Thoroughly understand the role of ports in international trade and transport and how ports can benefit or detract from the economics development of countries and their sea-borne trade.

Understand the effect of globalisation on port choice and how changes in logistics and distribution patterns influence the development or decline of ports.

Be aware of the location of major world ports in liner, dry bulk and liquid trades.

Understand the geographic reasons for port location and the extent to which this may depend on the nature of their hinterland and natural resources.

Understand the different types of ports and access to ports (natural, man made, river, estuary) and the diversity of specialist port operations.

Understand the enhanced role of ports in a through transport context – hub ports, feeder/transhipment ports, intermodal interfaces.

Be aware of the role of national, regional and local government in port provision.

Understand the different forms of the ownership structure of ports and of port services; public/private, landlord only, full or part service provider, terminal facilities within ports.

Be aware of the use of Free Port/Free Trade Zones as an economics tool.

SHIPS AND CARGOES

Thoroughly understand the fundamental differences between dry bulk cargo ships, general-purpose ships, liners (container, break-bulk and Ro-Ro) and tankers, including Ore/Oil and Ore/Bulk/Oil carriers. (Students may be expected to produce sketches).

Understand that Tankers sub-divide into several categories including carriers for crude-oil, petroleum products, chemicals, liquid gases, vegetable oils etc.

Be aware of size ranges of bulk-carriers including Capesize, Panamax, Handy-size.

Understand the purpose and basic design and construction features of decks, holds, hatches, derricks, winches cranes and other cargo handling gear.

Thoroughly understand the terminology of measuring ships including pseudo-tonnages – NT and GT. Actual tonnages – deadweight (dwat & dwcc) displacement (total and light). Capacities – bale cubic & grain cubic, TEU. Understand what information is contained in Stowage Plans.

Understand how particular ship types are required for the different cargoes and trade routes.

Thoroughly understand the basic characteristics of the main five commodities namely Coal, Ore, Grain, Fertilizers and Oil.

Be aware of the different sub-divisions within these categories.

Understand the hazards associated with the transport of certain commodities.

Understand the special requirements of unitised liner cargoes.

Understand the main places of origin and appropriate trade routes of other important cargoes plus any seasonal variations. Have a working knowledge of distances and voyage times.

A good grounding in maritime geography and access to an atlas is essential for this part of the syllabus.

PORT MANAGEMENT

Understand the basic rationale of port business.

Thoroughly understand how ports structure the delivery of services and the relationship between infrastructure, conservancy, navigation and handling facilities.

Understand how the activities are organised to interface with one another and typical port organisational structure.

Be aware of the importance of ports being managed as commercial enterprises irrespective of their ownership.

Thoroughly understand how port performance can be measured – vessel turn round time, cargo volume, speed of cargo handling, damage and pilferage prevention.

Be aware how quality management systems and benchmarking can improve performance.

Understand the responsibility for and nature of marine operations – conservancy, dredging, navigation aids, navigation control etc.

Understand the management of cargo operations on board and ashore. Understand the prime importance of avoiding traffic and cargo congestion.

Thoroughly understand the importance of safety management.

Thoroughly understand the importance of security to prevent terrorism, illegal immigration, theft and smuggling.

Understand the role of trade unions and other labour organisations including ITF.

Understand the role of statutory bodies – Customs, Immigration, Port Health, Marine Safety etc.

Understand and meet the needs of port users – shipowners and operators, ship agents, forwarders, truckers, rail and barge operators.

Thoroughly understand the information flow requirements of the port, statutory bodies and port users.

Understand how these are met by port community computer systems.

PORT COMPETITION AND MARKETING

Understand the nature of port competition, national and international.

Understand the need for market information including trade growth, vessel development, commercial needs and financial viability.

Thoroughly understand the relevance of geographic location to both vessel transit time and port rotation.

Understand the role of shipowners/ship operators, shippers/receivers, freight contractors, forwarders and other transport interests (eg railways, road hauliers).

Be aware of the various techniques of port promotion and how they assist with identification of potential users.

Understand the impact of inland transportation and inland depot/handling facilities.

Be aware of the scope for collaboration on through transport.

PORT PRICING

Thoroughly understand both the nature and types of port charges including those incorporating statutory navigational services, services to vessels, services to cargoes.

Understand the cost factors in pricing including for infrastructure, navigation services, equipment, staff and labour, marketing, security and safety and for environmental services.

Understand pricing policy specifically 'not for profit', government influenced, fully commercial.

Understand the effects of competition on pricing policy and how pricing is used as a tool to influence demand.

Understand the various factors used in establishing pricing structures including lengths of time included in base charge for vessels and cargo; units on which charges are based; simplicity of application and transparency; volume rebates.

Be aware of the various regulatory mechanisms including user appeals against charges.

Understand the integration of port charges with charges of other port operator and inland transport organisations and through transport charges.

LEGAL ASPECTS OF PORT MANAGEMENT

Be aware of the nature of port constitutions and the legal framework of ownership.

Be aware of Port laws and bye-laws, national legislation.

Be aware of the development of port facilities; the financing of port development.

Be aware of Laws relating to port security, operators liability and insurance.

Be aware of Laws and regulations relating to the employment of dockworkers.

Be aware of the freedom of port organisations to diversify their activities.

Be aware of development, ownership and control of Free Ports and Free Zones.

Be aware of the impact of international conventions on ports.

PORT PLANNING

Understand port development policy including the role of government, regional needs and competition.

Thoroughly understand planning principles and project planning and the role of traffic forecasts, analysis of demand factors, implications for marketing, involvement of users.

Thoroughly understand capacity calculations and the relationship between berth occupancy, service time and waiting time and also berth throughput.

Understand the principles behind port layout, physical constraints, terminal planning, specialised terminals, multipurpose terminals and support operations.

Understand the handling characteristics and requirements of break bulk, neo-bulk, special cargoes, dry bulk and liquid bulk commodities.

Understand flow analysis of cargo in a terminal and environmental factors and constraints.

PORT FINANCE

Understand the importance of financial management in port operating, specifically budgets, capital and revenue expenditures and investment appraisal.

Be aware of the importance of financial and commercial objectives including the analysis and monitoring of costs and port cost accounting.

Understand the need for a corporate analysis of financial data and for budgetary planning and control.

Be aware of project evaluation and review techniques and the capital budgeting and also the financial and economic appraisal of port investment proposals and traffic forecasting.

Be aware of joint venture opportunities for financing or management and policies for both common and sole user terminals.

PORT EQUIPMENT

Understand what is meant by port buildings, transit sheds, warehouses, maintenance workshops, amenity buildings, offices for port users etc.

Understand the different cargo handling equipment, types, their costs and the need for maintenance management.

Understand how future changes in vessel size and cargo handling techniques will compact on procurement and materials management.

PORT OWNERSHIP

Be aware of the different types of ownership including national or local government owned and managed, other public sector-owned ports and port trusts and the trend towards deregulation of ports.

Be aware of the transfer of party from state to private ownership, methods of privatisation; sale of shares, management and employee buyouts.

Understand what is meant by private sector owned ports including the different types of ownership i.e. outright, public sector ownership of port infrastructure combined with private sector provision, public ownership of port superstructure with private management and/or operation and the associated issues of lease contracts and joint ventures.

Order Form — TutorShip

Shipping guides LTD
The Port Information Specialists

This voucher entitles the student to a £10 discount off the price of *The Ships Atlas*. This offer is only available through Shipping Guides Ltd. Please contact us at the address below to find out the current price or visit our website www.portinfo.co.uk.

Company:
Address:

Post/Zip Code: 　　　　Country:

VAT No. 　　　　(EC only)
Contact: 　　　　Title:
Tel No: 　　　　Fax:
Email:

SHIPPING GUIDES LIMITED
75 Bell Street, Reigate, Surrey,
RH2 7AN, United Kingdom

Tel: +44 1737 242255
Fax: +44 1737 222449

Email: sales@portinfo.co.uk
Telex: 917070 Shipg G

VAT Registration Number
GB 243 9546 43

Nature of business

○ Ship master 　○ Ship owner/operator/manager 　○ Ship broker/agent

○ Ship charterer 　○ Legal services 　○ Financial services 　○ Other

If other, please specify:

Required Products

Product Name	Quantity	Price
The Ships Atlas		
	Subtotal	
	Postage	
	VAT	
	Total	

Please note that prices may be subject to VAT

Order Details

○ Please send a (proforma) invoice 　○ We have arranged direct payment to your bank 　○ We wish to pay by cheque/bank draft/credit card

(Delete as applicable)

The amount of £ 　Customers within the EU should quote their VAT numbers where appropriate

Please note that prices may be subject to VAT

Amex ○ 　Mastercard ○ 　Visa ○ 　Delta ○ 　Switch ○

Cardholder's Name:
Card Number:
Expiry Date: 　／
Signature: 　　　　Date: 　／　／

Method of payment

1. Sterling bank draft drawn on a bank in the UK made payable to Shipping Guides Ltd.
2. Credit card (complete section left).
3. Direct payment in Pounds Sterling to our bank (details below). Payment to be made in full
   - All charges to your account
   - All direct payments to state company name and complete address

Our Bank Details
Barclays Bank plc,
90 - 92 High Street, Crawley,
West Sussex, RH10 1BP, UK.

Account Number: 30079332
Sort Code: 20-23-97
IBAN No: GB32 BARC 202397 30079332
Swiftcode: BARCGB22